ANTIQUE AND CLASSIC CARS, THEIR MAINTENANCE AND OPERATION

ANTIQUE
and
CLASSIC
CARS

Their Maintenance and Operation

BY

Richard C. Wheatley
and Brian Morgan

With drawings by
R. F. Neale

Bentley Publishers
1734 Massachusetts Avenue
Cambridge MA 02138

BENTLEY PUBLISHERS® | Automotive Reference™

Bentley Publishers, a division of Robert Bentley, Inc.
1734 Massachusetts Avenue
Cambridge, MA 02138 USA
800-423-4595 / 617-547-4170

Information that makes the difference®

BentleyPublishers®.com

First published in the United States of America, 1964
Revised edition 1976

Library of Congress Catalog Card Number 75-37230
ISBN 978-0-8376-0203-5
Job Code: X003-01

This paper used in this publication is acid free and meets the requirements of the National Standard for Information Sciences-Permanence of Paper for Printed Library Materials ♾

Printed in the United States of America

PREFACE

SOME four years ago we wrote a manual of instruction on the restoration of Vintage motor-cars from a state of semi-decay to something possibly a little better than their new condition. That book took the reader right through a complete overhaul up to the point where his car was ready to start its life all over again. Although we were determined not to describe anything of which we had no practical experience, we found that considerable condensation was required to keep this previous volume to manageable proportions and, therefore, only essentials were included. Even these, in many cases, were touched upon but briefly.

In this our second book we have sought not only to carry the story on from where we left it previously and to take the reader out onto the road with his car, but to retrace our steps in places and to cover more fully some of the points which we could merely outline before. In addition to the purely technical side of motor-car ownership we have mentioned some of the enjoyable occasions on which a Vintage or Thoroughbred car is the correct wear and paid a tribute to the various organisations who arrange that these occasions do occur.

The joys of motoring in a Vintage car are not to be measured by mere performance, they have an entity quite different to anything produced today. Some models are not even sluggards judged by present standards and certain early makes, without the encumbrance of four-wheel brakes and heavy axles, had a precision of steering which has never been surpassed.

There is immense pleasure to be obtained from driving a car with a long-stroke engine and a high axle ratio, and in mastering the difficulties of a crash gear-box. It is also a pleasant thought that you have a vehicle which if well maintained does not depreciate in value.

We sincerely believe that every man is the better for practising a hobby in which, when earning his living is over for the day, he can become sufficiently deeply engrossed that cares of office become forgotten for a while. If the following pages help a few to enjoy their hobby still further then we shall be very content.

Birmingham, R.C.W.
January, 1964 B.M.

CONTENTS

CONTENTS

ACKNOWLEDGMENT

The Authors and Publishers would like to record their thanks to the following:

Michael M. Usher for his help with Chapter XI

Gordon G. McDonald for his help with Chapter XII

Graham S. Madeley for his help with Chapter XIV

Saga Services, 8 Oxford Road, Birmingham 13, for permission to reproduce Plates V, XII and XIII

Roger McDonald, District Bank House, Congleton, Cheshire, for permission to reproduce Plate VIII

Studio 3, Fitzroy Yard, Kingstown St., London N.W.1., for permission to reproduce Plate IX

Auto Tempo Meter Co. Ltd., 140 Kings Cross Road, London W.C.1, for permission to reproduce Plate III

Smith's Motor Accessories Ltd., 50 Oxgate Lane, London N.W.2, for permission to reproduce Plate IV and Fig. 14

Mrs. E. M. Burke for doing all the typing and secretarial work

LIST OF ILLUSTRATIONS

THE PLATES

DRAWINGS IN THE TEXT

CHAPTER 1

MOTOR VEHICLE REGULATIONS

MANY books have already been written describing Vintage and Thoroughbred cars, their peculiarities both of design and behaviour and their detailed technical specifications. We have given a few suggestions on making the choice of which car to own in our previous book[1] and so we will not cover old ground by repeating such information here. We assume that you will by now either have acquired a car in mint condition, or by a great expenditure of effort and skin and also not a little gold, restored one to its original beauty.

Before taking the car on the road there are certain formalities to be carried out of which the most important is the purchase of a Road Fund Licence; this however will not be issued until you have a Ministry of Transport Certificate of Roadworthiness and a Certificate of Insurance. Before you can obtain either of the above certificates your motor-car must comply with the Motor Vehicle (Construction and Use) Regulations. This verbal labyrinth is a masterpiece of confused thinking, obscure phraseology and inability to marshal the facts in any sane order.

After exhaustive exploration of the many relevant and irrelevant regulations and amendments we have extracted the following requirements; these are the most important regulations which apply to Vintage and Thoroughbred motor-cars at the present date. You can of course obtain the complete set of regulations and amendments from your local branch of H.M. Stationery Office.

Regulations for Motor-Cars

Brakes

Every motor-car must be equipped with an efficient braking system or efficient braking systems in either case having two means of operation. These shall be so designed and constructed that notwithstanding the failure of any part (other than a fixed member or a brake shoe anchor pin) through, or by means of, which the force necessary to apply the brakes is transmitted, there shall still be available for application by the driver to not less than half the number of wheels of the vehicle, brakes sufficient under the most adverse conditions to bring the vehicle to rest within a reasonable distance. The application of one means of operation shall not

[1] *The Restoration of Vintage and Thoroughbred Cars* Batsford, 1957.

affect or operate the pedal or hand lever of the other means of operation. All the brakes of a motor-car which are operated by one of the means of operation shall be capable of being applied by direct mechanical action without the intervention of any hydraulic, electric or pneumatic device. A motor-car with four wheels must be equipped with a braking system which can be set so as effectually to prevent two at least of the wheels from revolving when the vehicle is left unattended.

The above regulation applies only to motor-cars with four wheels.

The braking systems and means of operation, also all of the steering gear, must at all times while the motor-car is used on the road be maintained in an efficient working order and must be properly adjusted.

Tires

All the wheels of a motor-car, the unladen weight of which exceeds one ton, must be equipped with pneumatic tires except a motor-car of the above weight registered before 2nd January 1933, in which case it must be fitted with pneumatic tires or tires of soft or elastic material. All the tires of a motor-car must at all times while used on the road be maintained in such condition as to be free from any defect which might in any way cause damage to the surface of the road or danger to persons on or in the vehicle or to other persons using the road.

Wings

A motor-car must be provided with wings or other similar fittings to catch, as far as practicable, mud or water thrown up by the rotation of the wheels, except in the case of a vehicle in an unfinished condition proceeding to a works for completion.

Reverse Gear

Every motor-car which exceeds 8 cwt. unladen weight must be capable of being driven either forward or backward.

Windscreen

The windscreen of all motor-cars must be fitted with safety glass, and this and all other glass or transparent material must be maintained in such condition that it does not obscure the vision of the driver.

Windscreen Wiper

An efficient automatic windscreen wiper must be fitted to every motor-car unless the windscreen can be opened in such a way that the driver has an adequate view to the front without looking through the glass. The wiper must be maintained in efficient working order.

Driving Mirror

Every motor-car must be equipped either internally or externally with a mirror so that the driver can study any traffic, particularly police cars, to his rear.

Speedometer

Every motor-car registered on or after 1st October 1937 must be fitted with a speed indicator, accurate within a margin of plus or minus ten per cent, and this instrument must at all times be maintained in good working order.

Horn

An instrument to give audible and sufficient warning of approach must be fitted and at all times be maintained in efficient working order. This instrument must not be a siren, gong or bell.

Silencer

Every motor-car propelled by an internal combustion engine must be fitted with a silencer or expansion chamber capable of reducing the noise of the exhaust as far as possible; the vehicle must also be in such condition as to prevent the emission of avoidable smoke. Sleeve valve enthusiasts beware. If you are using solid fuel you must have an efficient appliance to prevent ashes and cinders from falling on to the horse road.

Side Lamps

Every motor-car must be equipped with two lamps, having electric bulbs of not more than 7 watts, or the equivalent in some other means of illumination, and fitted with frosted glass or other diffusing material capable of showing a white light to the front and fitted in such a way that no part of the vehicle projects more than 12 in. beyond the centre of the lamp on that side. The centres of the lamps must not be more than 5 ft. from the ground and both lamps must be the same height.

Rear Lamps

Every motor-car must be equipped with two lamps, having electric bulbs of at least 6 watts, or the equivalent in some other means of illumination, capable of showing a red light to the rear. The illuminated area of the lamp must be not less than a 2-in. diameter circle or if not circular of the same area as a 2-in. diameter circle and of such a shape that a circle of 1 in. diameter may be inscribed therein. The maximum height of the highest part of the lamp from the ground is 3 ft. 6 in. and the position must not be more than 30 in. from the extreme rear of the vehicle, the minimum distance between the lamps must be 21 in. and the maximum projection of the widest part of the vehicle beyond the nearest part of the lamp 24 in. Both lamps are to be the same height from the ground. The wiring must be in parallel so that failure of the bulb in one lamp will not result in cessation of supply to the other lamp. There is no minimum height for the rear lamps fitted to cars registered before 1st October 1954.

Reflectors

Every motor-car must be equipped with two red reflectors facing to the rear, each reflecting area must be not less than a 1½-in. diameter circle and if not circular at least of the same area as a 1½-in. diameter circle and of such shape that a circle of 1 in. diameter may be inscribed therein and capable of being contained within a circle of 6 in. diameter. The maximum height of the highest part of the reflectors from the ground is 3 ft. 6 in. and the minimum height of the lowest part 1 ft. 3 in.; they must not be fitted more than 30 in. from the extreme rear of the vehicle. The minimum distance between the reflectors must be 21 in. and the maximum projection of the widest part of the vehicle beyond the nearest part of the reflector 16 in. Both reflectors must be the same height from the ground, in a vertical position and facing squarely to the rear.

The exceptions to the regulations with regard to all lamps are that if they are blanked off so that they cannot be used or if they are constructed to be illuminated by an electric bulb but there is no supply of power in the car for this purpose, then they can be in any position that you choose and you do not need reflectors but it will be better for your health, and your pocket, if you do not take the car on the road after dark.

Headlamps and Foglamps

These are front lamps having a power of more than 7 watts and should be mounted with their centres not more than 3 ft. 6 in. above the road and, except in the case of a lamp used in fog or a snow-storm, not less than 2 ft. 2 in. from the ground. No lamps of this type may be used unless such lamps are so constructed that:

(*a*) The beam of light is permanently deflected downwards so that with the vehicle on level ground a person who is more than 25 ft. away from the vehicle and whose eye level is not less than 3 ft. 6 in. from the ground (what a funny little man) will not be dazzled, or

(*b*) The lamps are fitted with a dipping mechanism so that the beam of light can be deflected downwards, or downwards and to the left, so that a person standing in the position as at (*a*) will not be dazzled, or

(*c*) That the lamps can be switched off and at the same time another lamp switched on which complies with (*a*).

Reversing Lights

A reversing light must be illuminated by an electric bulb and the power must not exceed 24 watts. It must be so fitted that the beam of light is incapable of dazzling a person who is standing on the same horizontal plane as the vehicle at a greater distance than 25 ft. from the light and whose eye level is not less than 3 ft. 6 in. above the plane (the same little man—he must be an employee of the Ministry of Transport suffering from Duck's disease).

The light must be either switched on automatically by the selection of the reverse gear or by the operation of a switch by the driver of the vehicle. On motor-cars registered before 1st July 1954 this switch does not have to be provided with a warning indicator to show if the light is on but we think it is advisable to have an indicator as it is so easy to leave the light on by mistake which, of course, is illegal and a great inconvenience to other road users.

Markings of Electric Bulbs

Every electric light bulb in a lamp must have the wattage indelibly marked on the glass or on the metal cap.

Rear Plate Illumination

The rear number plate must be illuminated during the hours of darkness.

Mascots

No mascot may be carried on a motor-car registered on or after 1st October 1937 in any position where it is likely to strike any person with whom the vehicle may collide unless the mascot is not liable to cause injury to such person by reason of any projection thereon. Apparently you are allowed to spike pedestrians with your vintage Hispano stork but that doesn't mean to say that you won't have an action for damages brought against you by the spiked one.

Towing

No motor vehicle shall tow any other vehicle unless the tow rope be so adjusted that the distance separating the nearest points of the two vehicles shall not exceed 15 ft. and steps must be taken to render the tow rope easily distinguishable by other users of the road.

Television Sets

No person may use or install for use in a motor vehicle a television receiving apparatus if the screen is visible to the driver whilst in the driving seat or if the controls thereof other than the sound volume control are within his reach. So you can stop trying to fit that 21-in. screen into your new dashboard layout.

The foregoing covers all the necessary regulations applicable to Vintage and Thoroughbred cars. There is a delightful little paragraph dealing with lavatory basins and closets but since it is unlikely that you will have these fitted at the moment, and it will not be necessary until the farmers have removed all the trees and hedges, we will not bother you with the gruesome details.

Ministry of Transport Vehicle Test

All Vintage and Thoroughbred cars must now pass the above test if they are to be used on the road and, since Examiners have the power to refuse tests in certain circumstances, for your own sake it is advisable to make sure when you submit your car for test:

(*a*) That you have the log book with you.

(*b*) That the motor-car is not so dirty as to make the examination too difficult.

(*c*) That the motor-car contains oil, petrol and water if necessary.

As you cannot tax the car before having it examined, you are allowed by the authorities to drive your car to and from the testing station unlicensed. Do not tempt providence by extending this journey to include the local pub on your way home from a successful passing of the test.

The following are the requirements for the examination.

Brakes

The brakes must comply with the Motor Vehicle (C and U) Regulations as aforementioned.

The braking cables or rods must be in good condition, they must be working freely and they must not chafe on other parts of the vehicle. Bolts and clevis pins must not be excessively worn and they must be effectively secured by nuts or split pins where these are used.

Hydraulic systems must be free from visible leaks in pipes and cylinders, there must be no chafing of flexible pipes or pipe lines on other parts of the vehicle, the system must be free from air causing sponginess, and it must be properly adjusted.

Handbrake pawls and ratchets must not be excessively worn and must hold the lever securely in any position. Foot pedals and hand levers must have an adequate reserve of travel when fully applied. Brake drums and hubs must be free from oil leakage which might be affecting the brake linings. There must be no lack of balance in the application of the brakes which would cause, or be likely to cause, serious pulling to one side. There must be no other defect in the vehicle or its equipment by reason of which the braking requirements are not complied with.

The regulations require the examination of the braking systems to include a test of the efficiency of the brakes, and this may be carried out by driving the motor-car on the road, applying its brakes, and using a decelerometer to measure the braking efficiency. The test should not be carried out at a speed of more than 20 m.p.h. Alternatively a roller or platform type of brake testing apparatus may be used.

The minimum percentage efficiencies are as follows:

Motor-cars with either or both brake systems operating on four wheels.	
A four-wheel brake (this is usually the footbrake)	50%
A second brake (this is usually the handbrake)	25%
Motor-cars with both brake systems operating on two wheels.	
One brake (this is usually the footbrake)	30%
A second brake (this is usually the handbrake)	25%

If the tester thinks it necessary he may carry out a supplementary test by driving the motor-car to find out whether it complies with the regulations other than for a percentage braking efficiency.

Steering

The steering requirements are the same for all vehicles. The track rod, steering arm and all ball and other joints in steering arms and drag links must be in good condition and free from excessive stiffness or wear. All securing nuts and split pins must be in position. The steering box must be securely mounted, there must be no excessive wear or stiffness in the king pins and bushes or in the wheel bearings. There must not be any excessive play or slackness in the system as indicated by free movement at the steering wheel, nor must there be any restriction of movement. There must be no defect in any part of the steering mechanism likely to affect its efficiency.

Lighting Equipment and Reflectors

Headlamps, fog lamps, side lamps, rear lamps and reflectors must comply with the requirements of the Motor Vehicle (C and U) Regulations with the exception of the case dealt with earlier in this chapter. If you wish to have further details, the regulations for the test and a tester's manual can be obtained from H.M. Stationery Office, but if your motor-car is in good condition it should pass the test easily.

Insurance Engineer's Examination

When you apply for insurance you will, of course, fill in the proposal form but the insurance company will also probably require an engineer's report on the condition of your car. The examination will consist of visual inspection of the following details. The steering gear for wear and fractures; the wheels for general condition and strength of spokes on wire wheels and also soundness of attachment of the wheels to the hubs. The tires will be examined for condition of tread sufficient to prevent skidding, the wheel bearings for looseness, the road springs for broken leaves or lack of "set", and the electric wiring for proper insulation and for proximity to the fuel system. The brake actuating mechanism must have freedom of movement, the throttle linkage must be secure and correctly positioned for the return spring to close the throttle if the linkage should break. The general condition of the under-carriage will be examined particularly for freedom from rust and fracture and the windscreen for being fitted with safety glass. The engineer may also wish to drive the motor-car on the road and so you will have to get a Road Fund Licence. To enable you to obtain this the insurance company will issue you with a cover note but should the engineer's report be unsatisfactory the insurance policy and certificate will not be issued until the faults have been rectified.

The engineer, when road testing the motor-car, will examine the following points. Both systems of braking must be in efficient working order and properly balanced, the transmission must have all gears in working order and the back axle must not be unduly noisy. Satisfactory action of the ignition switch, free movement of the steering and stability of the car when running will be checked.

If all the foregoing tests and examinations have been concluded satisfactorily, and you now have all the necessary licences and certificates, the great day will have arrived to take the car for its initial run. Probably the first time you park your motor-car some clot will be there who will gape at the car in a dim sort of way and then make the usual somewhat obvious remark "They don't make 'em like that now Mister". We have never been quite sure if this remark is meant to be complimentary or not. However, you will find that the reply that brings this opening gambit to a firm conclusion, and which is equally ambiguous, is "No, they cor get the stuff".

CHAPTER II

DRIVING AND THE USE OF THE CONTROLS

WHILE there is great pleasure in driving a Vintage or Thoroughbred car it is most important to realise the limitations of your particular model. Vintage touring cars should be driven on a conservation of momentum principle rather than the modern flat-out acceleration and then stand on the brakes style. You cannot expect this type of car to be as lively as a small modern saloon but you can nevertheless get great enjoyment out of driving it provided that you are in the right frame of mind to use it properly, within its limitations. For instance, a Vauxhall 30/98 and a Rolls-Royce Phantom II Continental in good condition would have about the same maximum speeds, but to get the greatest pleasure from driving them you will need a different style and frame of mind for each car. Get used to changing up at much lower engine revolutions and keep going in top gear until much lower speeds have been reached when climbing hills than when driving a modern car, as most Vintage engines develop their power at lower speeds than their modern counterparts. While this does not necessarily apply to Vintage and Thoroughbred sports cars, even they will travel slowly and accelerate extremely well in top gear compared with the modern versions. In most cases the older engines are slower revving and your driving, therefore, must be in harmony with this characteristic. There is no doubt that a Vintage or Thoroughbred car must be in first class condition if it is to be worth driving. Therefore if you notice anything wrong, however small, do correct the fault at the earliest possible moment as otherwise you will gradually get tired of the car.

Gear Changing

If your car is a Vintage model it will almost certainly be fitted with a crash gear-box and in this case double-declutching is the only satisfactory method, in normal circumstances, of changing up and down. To mesh the gears silently they must be running at the correct speeds and before the advent of the synchromesh gear mechanism this depended entirely on the skill of the driver, and such dexterity can only be obtained by practice. The sequence of operations for changing up is as follows. Having engaged first gear, accelerate until the desired speed is reached then close the throttle, disengage the clutch and move the gear-lever into neutral all simultaneously. Next, with the throttle still closed, re-engage the clutch and pause until the clutch shaft is at the correct speed and then again disengage and at the same time move the lever into second gear. Re-engage the clutch and accelerate, repeating for the other gears. When disengaging the clutch use the full movement of the pedal. This series of movements will become very smooth and fast with practice and should result in an absolutely silent gear change. The pause in neutral is not always of the same duration as this varies with the speed of the car and the difference in ratio of the gears to be engaged. When the rhythm of this operation has been learned so as to become automatic, a change at exactly the same speed and rhythm can be executed without using the clutch at all, but do this gently at first. Another method of upward gear change is what we will call the snatch or racing change. In this case the throttle is kept wide open while the clutch is disengaged and the gear lever moved from one gear to the next but the movements must be very rapid and the timing exact. If there is any hesitation the result may be catastrophic. Your car may be fitted with a clutch stop—a device so constructed as to come into operation when the clutch pedal is fully depressed, when it acts as a brake and slows down the spinning clutch shaft. It can be adjusted to be either fierce or mild in action. It is very useful for slowing down the gears on engagement when the car is at rest, but otherwise it is rather an undesirable feature. It may be a necessary evil on some cars when used for competition work but it must never come into operation when executing a downward change and it is therefore better to set it to be mild in action. It is, of course, designed to make much faster upward changes.

In downward gear changes on crash gear-boxes the double-declutch method is absolutely essential; the procedure is as follows. Disengage the clutch, close the throttle and move the gear lever into neutral, all these movements to be performed simultaneously. Then re-engage the clutch, accelerate the engine until the clutch shaft is running at the right speed when the throttle should be closed, the clutch should be disengaged and the gear lever pushed into the lower gear. Re-engage the clutch and accelerate. When you can execute this series of movements rapidly, and with complete precision, they can be speeded up by keeping the throttle open all the time and when done perfectly this sounds and feels magnificent and will give you a great sense of achievement. It is also possible to carry out the downward changes without using the clutch, but these are much more dangerous than upward clutchless changes due to no hesitation being permissible.

Ignition Control

Most Vintage cars were fitted with manual ignition control but the manipulation of this control is not so necessary now as when the car was built, due to the improved anti-detonating quality of modern fuels and the engine probably having a very low compression ratio unless it has been modified. Leave the control in the fully advanced position as much as possible except for starting when the ignition should be at full retard. However, remember that if you have magneto ignition then the spark is much stronger at full advance than in the retarded position: there is no difference with coil ignition. Retard the ignition only sufficiently to prevent pinking or when driving at very low speeds. If you have a high compression engine more discretion must be used. A rough guide is to operate the control between the half-way position and full advance, so that you get the best performance without pinking pro rata with the r.p.m. of the engine.

Mixture Control

There is usually some type of mixture control fitted to the car to facilitate starting. This device is often a flap or shutter fitted to the carburetter air intake to increase the suction on the jet and so to give a rich mixture. There are also moveable jets for this purpose, but remember always to return this control to the normal running position as soon as possible after the engine has started.

Some cars were also fitted with a mixture control, not only for starting, but to vary the mixture while the car is running. A strong mixture is for acceleration and hill climbing and a weak one for economy. In this case you will have to find out by trial and error the best position of the control for the type of performance you require at the time. Certain cars were also fitted with Kigass, which is merely a pump to force atomised petrol into the induction manifold to give an easy start. The pump should be screwed down tightly immediately after use to prevent the engine sucking itself full of neat petrol.

Brakes

If your motor-car is fitted with two-wheel brakes only, you will have to be careful in present-day traffic, especially as modern cars are apt to pass you and then pull in and brake violently. Four-wheel brake systems should be satisfactory but will need more pedal pressure than modern versions. Should your car have a transmission brake care should be taken in its use, as some of them are very fierce and are likely to cause skidding on a greasy surface. Use such a brake mainly for parking.

When filling up with petrol remember that high grade petrol in a low compression engine is a waste of money—the low grade fuel will give you just as good a performance. Always keep the radiator well filled with soft water and the engine, gear-box and back axle topped up with oil.

CHAPTER III

MAINTENANCE OF THE RUNNING GEAR

IN the next few chapters we propose to deal with the maintenance of your car in a good roadworthy condition and we shall speak of a different section of the car in each chapter. As the years pass it will become increasingly difficult and expensive to get your Vintage or Thoroughbred motorcar looked after professionally and, in any case, as the ownership of such a vehicle is nowadays generally a hobby, the more of the work you can do yourself the more completely will you be indulging in your pastime. Let us say immediately for those who can afford it and have not the time to look after their car, that there are some very fine establishments where the work can be carried out impeccably; nevertheless, there is nothing quite so satisfying as to do the job yourself.

We would also like to emphasise that in the act of giving your motorcar its routine maintenance you will probably spot small detail defects far sooner than you would do merely by using the car and thus quite possibly avert expensive derangements at a later date. The above is particularly true in the case of cleaning your car and is probably the strongest argument for performing this chore yourself.

Just before getting down to details may we also say that we do not intend to go over the ground covered by our previous book, *The Restoration of Vintage and Thoroughbred Cars*, and in many instances where repair work is called for you may refer back to the earlier volume for more details.

Front Axle and Steering Gear

It seems logical to start the inspection at the front of your car so let us look first at the front axle, which in all probability will be the conventional beam. Before starting your inspection, jack up the axle so that the wheels are off the ground and then give the whole assembly a good clean. Proceed to check the tightness of the bolts which secure the axle to the springs as these have a way of slowly coming loose even with the best of locking devices. This is partly caused by the bolts stretching and general bedding down of the springs. If there are any doubtful bolts or nuts you will of course replace them immediately. While you are at this point check that the axle is located at the right point on the springs and that it has not moved forwards or backwards, due to your having run one of the front wheels into an obstruction. It will generally be obvious if the axle has moved because the centre pin of the spring will no longer be over the centre of the axle. In such a case the locating spigot of the spring will no longer be attached to the spring, or its register in the axle is elongated, and repairs are called for.

Moving out now to either end of the axle we come to the king pins. First test these for play by grasping the road wheel at top and bottom and rocking it inwards at the top and outwards at the bottom at the same time watching the movement of the stub axle relative to the axle beam. It is important if the wheel does rock that you differentiate between wheel bearing looseness and play in the king pin, hence the reason for looking at the right point when making the test. More than $\frac{3}{16}$ in. play at the top of the wheel, if the hub bearings are sound, definitely calls for treatment of the king pins and bushes.

If this test reveals that there is play in the hubs then you must first ascertain whether your car has ball, roller or taper roller races at this point. With ball or roller races there should be no play at all and, if there is any play, then either the races need replacement or they are loose either on the stub axle or in the hub. Practically every known size of ball or roller race is readily obtainable from one of the well-known manufacturers if the size is quoted or a sample submitted; they will not, however, know the size of front hub race fitted to the 1923 Targa Florio model Nebbiolo—so always quote the size. With taper roller races a certain amount of play is necessary and they are normally adjustable by means of the retaining nut on the end of the stub axle. If you have no definite instructions as to how much play your hub should have, take the adjustment up until there is just no play and then take the nut back one sixth of a turn. All hub races should be grease lubricated with a high melting point hub grease about every 10,000 miles, when the hubs should be removed and all the old grease washed out and the races repacked. While doing this examine the oil seals, although it will be fairly obvious to see if these are working correctly by noticing whether any lubricant leaks out when the car has been used. We find "Oiline Hub Grease" very good as it is particularly stable and does not overtax the sealing qualities of the Vintage felt washers which are not so good at holding-in some of the more fluid modern greases.

If you are happy with your king pins they can now be lubricated, and it is fairly certain that this will be done via a grease nipple. The number of cars one sees with battered old grease nipples would make one think that such items were hard to obtain instead of them being in stock at nearly every garage. Once a nipple is damaged or choked it is useless and so it is a good idea to keep a few in stock and as soon as there is any difficulty in getting the lubricant through, or if the joint between the gun and the nipple leaks, whip it out and put in a new one. Always lubricate the king pins with the weight of the car off the front wheels to allow fresh lubricant to get onto the load-carrying faces.

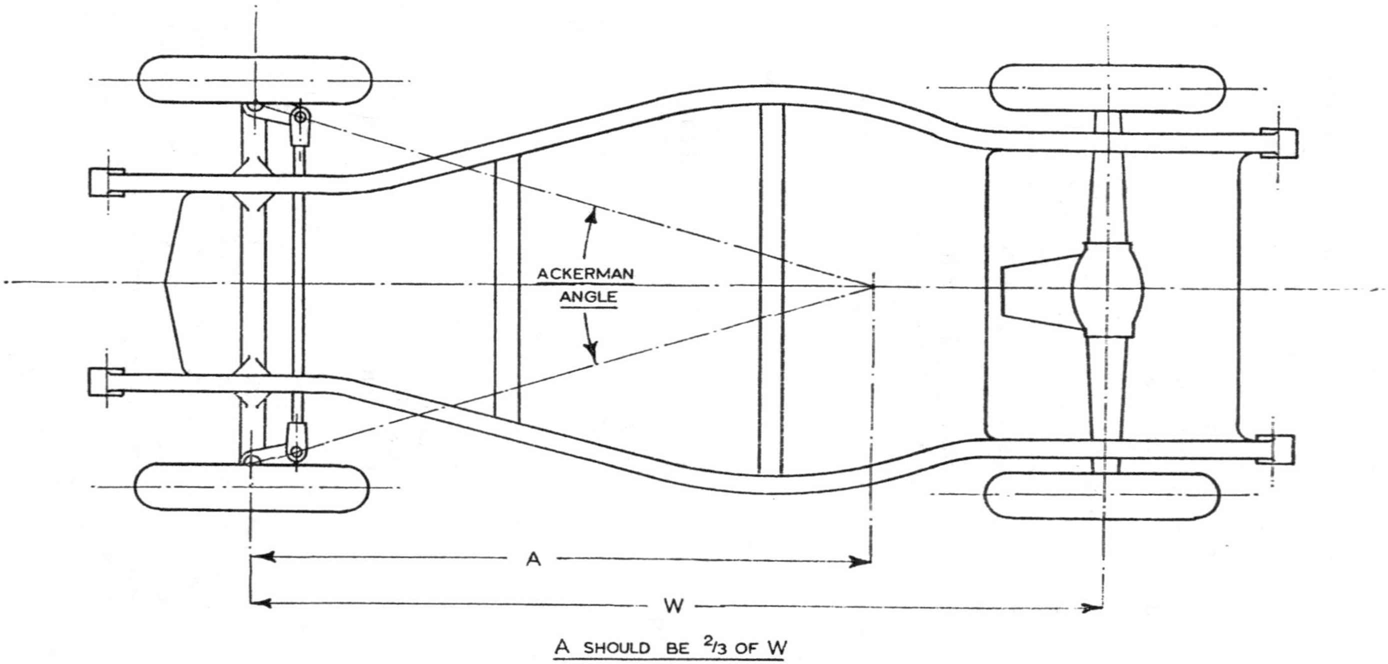

1 *Correct setting of steering arms*

For what it is worth we recommend the use of very heavy oil for all chassis lubrication other than hubs, as its lubricating and preservative qualities are far higher than those of any grease. For *concours* competitors it has the disadvantage of leaking out of all the joints and having to be wiped off but, after all, you can always leave your maintenance other than cleaning until after the concours.

Some early cars will be fitted with Stauffer grease-cups and in such cases grease must be used. This should be of the lightest variety, but it should be remembered that grease does not flow in the same way as heavy oil. For this reason attention is required more frequently and, in any case, always give your grease-cups a turn after a wet journey.

The next step is to look at the steering arms attached to the stub axles. These are liable to get bent if you run into an obstruction and usually it will be obvious if one of them is faulty. If you are doubtful on this point and want to check their correct angle you can do it in the way illustrated in fig. 1. It will be seen that a straight line or tight string passing through the king pin centre and the centre of the steering pivot on the arm will also pass through the centre line of the chassis (probably the propeller shaft) at a point two-thirds of the wheel base of the car away from the front axle.

Now move the front wheels over the complete range of their steering arc and see that they move freely. Stiffness may indicate lack of lubrication in the various ball joints, or even in the steering box, so attend to this first. If the stiffness is still there you must find out what is the cause, as it may mean that something is breaking up. The easiest method is to isolate each section of the steering linkage by detaching the necessary ball joint and tracking down the cause of the trouble. The same procedure applies if there is excessive play in the steering gear, but often you can find the points of free movement by getting someone else to move the steering wheel lightly backwards and forwards with the front wheels on the ground and watching each joint in turn. Take up any play in the steering joints but be sure that they are still perfectly free on both of the full lock positions. Ovality in the ball joints will eventually render it impossible to get no play in the straight ahead position and then replacement will have to be carried out.

It is as well to keep all the steering linkage clean, so that during your routine maintenance you can visually examine the various parts for dents and cracks. Realising that the steering is the most vital of all your controls, if you find anything doubtful put it right straight away. At least once a year check the toe-in of the front wheels; here again there will be a recommendation for your particular motor-car but if you do not know what the measurement should be, $\frac{1}{8}$ in. at the wheel rims will not be far out.

Moving back now to the steering box, first visually examine the attachment of the drop arm to its shaft and see that it is secure. Also check that in the straight ahead position the drop arm makes approximately a right angle with the drag link. If it does not, then in all probability the steering arm attached to the stub axle, onto which the drag link pivots, is bent, and your lock is being restricted at one end of the steering travel.

Keep the steering box topped up with the right oil or grease. We recommend heavy oil but if there are no seals on your box then you will have to use grease. Check the play in the actual box and the up and down play in the drop arm shaft. You may be able to take out a certain amount of free movement if the meshing is adjustable, but see that you still have perfect freedom of movement at the full lock positions. Do not neglect to oil the bearing at the top of the steering column and also, if you have the necessary adjustment, take out any endwise movement in the column itself.

Some cars, as they get old, develop front wheel wobble, which can be extremely frightening. To those who have never experienced this phenomenon let us say that it usually happens at low speeds but the result is no less devastating to your nerves. It is usually started by the front wheels going over irregularities in the road surface of just the right frequency, and then the steering wheel disappears into a blur as it madly oscillates from lock to lock. This peculiar behaviour is generally due either to the owner having fitted larger section tires than the maker stipulated, general wear and tear, to the castor action having been altered by tilting the axle on its springs or to the steering system having less frictional losses than when it was new. Incorrect toe-in can also promote wobbling. The cures are the reverse of the causes, viz; go back to narrow section tires or blow up the existing tires to a higher pressure, alter the castor angle or introduce some friction into the system. The latter can be done on some cars by removing the ball thrust races on the king pins and replacing them by plain thrust washers. Alternatively a steering damper can be fitted. Usually only a very small amount of friction, such as cannot even be felt at the steering wheel, is all that is necessary to cure this evil. The steering damper should be fitted to act on the track rod and is normally mounted on the front axle beam.

A last tip before passing on—be careful, when jacking up the front of a car fitted with bottom mounted brake camshafts, not to put the jack under these shafts instead of under the axle. They will never be the same again if you do.

Back Axle

Having finished your inspection of the front axle proceed now to jack up the back axle. Do not do this with a single jack under the centre of the axle unless you are quite sure that you have a one piece steel axle casing. Some light alloy casing centres will not stand this treatment, and in any case the car will be much more stable on two jacks.

First check the spring mounting bolts for tightness, as on the front axle, unless your car has cantilever or some other form of suspension. In such a case examine the mounting of the axle on the springs and see that all is well. Lubricate this point if it be necessary. Next turn each wheel by hand to see that it revolves freely and if it does not, and you are quite sure that the brakes are not rubbing, then further investigation will be necessary. Start the engine and let it drive the wheels in bottom gear. You can then see if the hubs are running true. If one of them is not then in all probability the axle shaft is bent, but if they are both apparently in truth, then only a process of dismantling and elimination of part by part will get you to the root of the trouble. When doing this always chock the front wheels for safety.

Check the play in the axle by locking the road wheels and rotating the propeller shaft by hand. If this is more than a few degrees and you feel that it warrants improvement, on no account start by meshing the pinion further into the crown wheel. This is a common mistake and it must be realised that the adjustment was provided by the makers to get the meshing right in the first place and not as a means of removing backlash.There is only one correct position for the adjustment and unless some previous owner has fiddled about unnecessarily then it is probably in the right place now. The only way to get rid of excessive play in any axle is to strip the axle down and to find out where the trouble lies and then to put that particular part into good condition again.

It is not a bad idea very occasionally to draw out your axle shafts and examine their splines. They sometimes gradually twist off and can let you down when least expected. Back axles are normally very reliable, but do not neglect to drain out the oil and refill about every 5,000 miles just because you are not having any trouble. At the same time examine the old oil for any signs of metal, as these may give you a clue of impending disaster before it actually happens and save you a mint of money. There is no need to use very heavy oil in back axles nowadays. With the exception of worm drives and hypoids, which need special oils, the normal axle will run happily on SAE 40 engine oil and SAE 140 is the absolute maximum viscosity to use. The lighter the oil the more of your expensive power gets to the back wheels.

One last tip—never run the back axle with only one wheel jacked up. The differential was never designed for this treatment and will not last for very long if you do.

The Braking System

Although the general efficiency of your braking system will be obvious every time that you drive the car, it is as well not to be lulled into a state of false security and to give the whole system a thorough going-over every six months. It is surprising how you can get used to a gradually diminishing rate of retardation and subconsciously adjust your driving accordingly, only to get caught out when someone in a modern heap decides to stand on everything when he is about six feet in front of you.

First jack up all four wheels of the car and remove all the wheels and brake drums. If you only end up by cleaning the drums free of all the old brake lining material it will be worth the trouble. Having examined the linings to see if they have plenty of life left in them, next get someone to work the brake pedal and see that all the brake shoes return to the fully off position each time the pedal is released. There are many elderly cars going around with all the brakes rubbing due to neglect, and not only do they not go so well in this condition, but also the brake drums are always hot and consequently the brakes are not so efficient as they might be when they are really needed. Clean all the operating mechanism and then lubricate the pivots and linkage connections. A good lubricant for clevis pins is molybdenum disulphide grease which lasts a long time but the pin must be dismantled to apply the grease. Other causes of stiffness in the system can be bent brake rods, seized cable pulleys, cross shafts tight in their bearings due to misalignment of the chassis frame, unlubricated Bowden cables or seized brake camshafts. Make sure that each part works freely before blaming the pull-off springs which, due to their light loading, generally last many years. On no account get out of your trouble by adding extra pull-off springs externally, this only makes the brakes harder to apply and if the system did not need them originally there is no need for them now. Many Vintage cars are spoilt by having a few old mattress springs as part of their braking layout. When you have everything working freely and still the shoes do not return properly, then you will have to fit new shoe-springs.

Do not over-oil the brake camshaft bearings, as if you do the oil will probably end up in the brake drum and you will be worse off than ever. See that the shoe operating mechanism, probably a cam, is not nearly at the end of its movement. If it is, and the linings are still full of life, then you will either have to build up the ends of the shoes or fit thicker linings, which will then have to be bedded down to the shape of the drum.

When all the system is working to your satisfaction, including the hand-brake mechanism, look at the working surfaces of the drums. If these are badly scored they will never work very well and should be skimmed or linered or some drums in better condition sought for and fitted.

If there is oil on the linings there is only one way in which to remove it satisfactorily, and that is to take it to someone who has a trichlorethylene degreaser. Treatment in such a plant will entirely remove oil or grease but any other method, such as cleaning in petrol, will not do more than make the oil penetrate even further into the lining.

So far we have been talking of mechanical braking systems. Hydraulic operation is relatively very much more simple, and certainly the system should not suffer from frictional losses. Examine all the pipework and particularly the flexible pipes. If the latter appear in any way perished or kinked discard them without hesitation. Elderly hydraulic brakes which have never had any renewals could possibly by now do with a complete new set of cup washers in both operating and master cylinders, and such spares are nearly all available from the makers. Do not regularly go round all the pipe connections with a spanner and give each one a further tighten just for luck. Treatment of this sort will eventually thin the end of the pipe to such an extent that it will break off. Rest content if you can see no sign of seepage at the joints and if the flexible pipes look in good condition. Always keep the reservoir topped up with the correct grade of fluid.

Coming now to the more exotic forms of brake application, you may have a vacuum servo motor. These are normally extremely reliable but, just make sure that the pipe connections are tight and put a few drops of engine oil down the air intake to lubricate the valve and operating cylinder. The most commonly found make of vacuum servo motor is Clayton Dewandre and all spares are available from the makers. Some cars are fitted with mechanical servo motors which again usually have a long and trouble free life. However, the day must come when these need relining, and you should also see that the operating linkage for such a mechanism is working freely and in correct adjustment. As such devices are very much in the minority and as the predominating design is very well covered in the instruction manual for that make, we will not go further into the matter here.

Having seen that the whole braking mechanism is working satisfactorily there only remains the adjustment. A great help here is to make a piece of wood that can be propped between the brake pedal and some fixed part of the car like the driving seat or the steering column and which will hold the pedal about one inch from the fully off position. You can then adjust your brakes individually so that each one gives the same amount of braking resistance knowing that all the backlash has been taken out under tension from the pedal. When the wood is removed all the drums should, of course, rotate freely. We cannot go into any details of all the vast number of systems and their individual peculiarities of adjustment, but the one golden rule is to see that all the operating levers make less than a right angle with their operating rods when the brakes are adjusted so that the linings are just not touching the drums (fig. 2). Any compensating devices should be in their mid-positions, and if the above conditions do not apply then either something is worn beyond the safe limit or the operating rods or cables have stretched and must be shortened or replaced.

Remember that with a mechanical servo motor the front brakes will probably be worked by the motor only and cannot be put on with the car at rest. Any sponginess in hydraulic systems is generally due to air bubbles in the pipes or cylinders and these must be bled at the points provided until a solid-feeling pedal is obtained.

Some Vintage cars have cross shafts which are very weak torsionally and the only way to get a balanced brake on all wheels is finally to take the car on the road and to adjust each brake individually until balance is achieved.

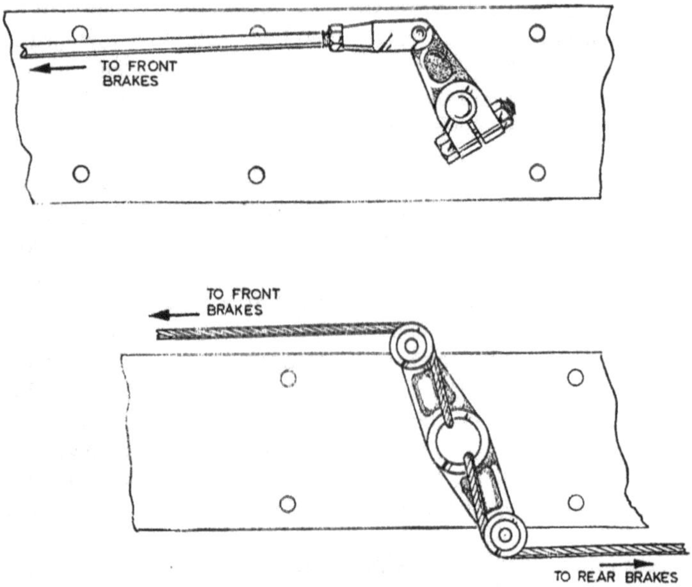

2 *Correct relative angle between lever and rod or cable with brakes in "off" position*

The Suspension

In nearly all cases the suspension will be by leaf springs and their maintenance can be carried out at the same time as you are attending to the axles. If your springs are ungaitered check for broken leaves. First clean the springs externally and then jack up the car under the frame to take the load off the springs and inject spring oil between the leaves to wash out all rust and dirt. Follow up with either thick oil diluted with petrol which will evaporate and leave a good film of oil between each leaf or put in molybdenum disulphide or graphite grease with a knife. With gaitered springs at least inspect the part which is visible for broken leaves and then lubricate through the nipples provided with thick oil. Grease is useless here as it will not penetrate throughout the whole spring. Should the gaiters not be provided with a means of lubrication then they must be removed about once a year and the springs oiled. A torn or damaged gaiter is worse than no gaiter at all as water will get in and probably not be able to get out again with consequential rusting of the spring.

There is no doubt that a well gaitered and lubricated leaf spring will give very long service without deterioration and if you do not want to go to the expense of gaiters, a substitute can be found in the more modern plastic tape. This is easily renewable after each lubrication. The last word in luxury is to take off the springs and to polish all their mating surfaces before lubricating and gaitering.

Should a leaf be fractured then it is advisable to take off both springs at that end of the car and send them to be repaired and reset, as when the spring on one side gets weak it cannot be long before you will have trouble with the other side. It is quite possible that old springs need setting up even though they are not actually broken, and if any of your springs have reached a point where their camber is reversed or the axle travel available has become very small then it is time to have them dealt with by a competent spring maker.

Lastly, as you lower the load of the car back onto each spring, watch for free movement at the shackle pins which will indicate whether they need attention. These should also be looked at for side play which can be cured by shimming and, of course, they should receive regular treatment from the grease or oil gun.

The shock absorbers may work either on the friction or the hydraulic principle. Both types will have pivots or rubber bushes in some part of their make up and these are subject to a good old hammering. Check the tightness of all mounting bolts, and if there is any free movement in the pivots they will not be going to last very much longer. It is essential that the connections between the axle and the damper and between the damper and the frame are all without play. If your friction dampers are made by André then you can get spares or replacements but other makes are now all obsolete. Probably the best course of action in the case of worn out obsolete makes is to replace them with new ones of André manufacture if repair seems impossible. The friction discs and spring star washers eventually all wear out but can easily be replaced. Check the balance of your friction dampers, occasionally equalising them on either side of the car. To do this you will have to detach one arm, say from the chassis frame, and slack back the adjustment until you can move the damper with a given load. A spring balance is a help in this operation as shown in fig. 3. Repeat on the other side of the car and attach the arms back onto their mountings. An equal number of turns on each adjuster will then give equal friction on each damper and they will be balanced—a condition which long service will have upset.

It is unfortunately a truth that nearly all the hydraulic dampers fitted to the cars about which we are writing are now worn beyond being of any use at all. They are exceedingly difficult for an amateur to recondition and unless you are lucky enough to find an unused set the only course of action open to you is to fit a set of modern dampers. Alternatively on cars with hard, small-movement suspension you can revert to friction dampers which will often give better results. If you suspect your hydraulic dampers, take off the operating arm from its connection to the axle and see if there is an appreciable resistance to fast movement by hand. If there is not then you will have to do something about it. Always consult the makers of any new shock absorbers before buying as they will recommend the correct type and setting for your particular car.

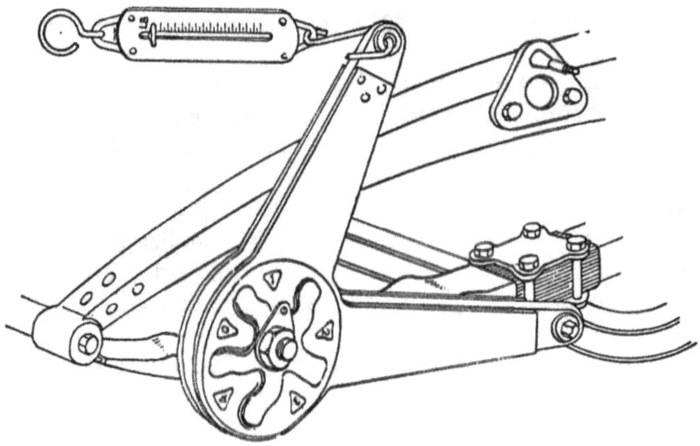

3 *Equalising the tension for Hartford shock absorbers by use of a spring balance*

The Road Wheels and Tires

Whenever the wheels are jacked clear of the ground do not miss the opportunity of spinning them by hand in order to see that they are running true. It is surprising how often one drives behind a proud owner in his otherwise pristine motor-car whose back wheel has every appearance of being on the point of departure from its hub. Should this be the case with one of your wheels then, if it is of the wire spoked variety, you can easily get it trued up by a specialist. Metal artillery or disc wheels are not easily straightened and it will be best in this case to make a search for one in better condition. Wooden wheels can be repaired by a wheelwright and although it may be surprising that such people still exist, in fact they do, often combining this trade with that of general blacksmith.

Wire wheels should be examined quite regularly for loose or broken spokes, as once the rot starts it quickly spreads. Rusty wire wheels often mar an otherwise good looking motor-car and if you do decide to have them repainted it is as well to consider whether or not to go the whole hog and have them respoked at the same time. Metal artillery wheels seldom give trouble but if any rust holes appear anywhere on one of yours then discard the wheel immediately. Wooden wheels suffering from loose spokes can be temporarily cured by soaking them in water but ultimately the only real cure is to visit the aforementioned wheelwright.

Check that the wheel mountings on the hubs are in good order. In these days of few punctures it is possible to go for long periods without having to remove the wheels and it is a good practice to remove them all, say every three months, and to change their position on the car diagonally (off front to near back and vice versa) and at the same time to see that their studs are firm in the hubs and that all screw threads are in good condition. With centre lock wheels take the opportunity to check the play in the splines by locking the hub and rotating the wheel back and forth. If the play is excessive the hubs and wheel centres need resplining. Occasionally wash out the splines with petrol and re-grease them keeping the lubricant away from the back taper but giving the taper on the locking ring a liberal dose. Ensure too that the locking ring has not come to the end of its thread before it pinches the wheel centre.

While you are changing the wheels round put each in turn on one front hub and check its balance. It must be remembered that wheels which are balanced when the tires are new will not necessarily remain in balance when the tire wears. Balanced wheels can make a great improvement to the steering of any car and on those capable of over 70 m.p.h. are an absolute necessity.

We hope that you will resist what to some people seems to be an irresistible temptation—to wit the fitting of tires of a larger section than those specified by the manufacturer. You will effect no improvement at all by doing this and will probably completely spoil the handling of your car. If you are in doubt as to the pressure at which your tires should be run most garages have a chart showing the correct pressure for any given section bearing a certain load and a quick visit to the local weighbridge to measure front and back axle loadings will give you the answer. If still in doubt err on the high side as the older cars with high geared steering become very hard work on low tire pressures and in any case the tires will always last longer if pumped up hard.

The Gear-box and Propeller Shaft

Both these items need very little attention apart from the routine topping-up of the gear-box and the lubrication of the joints on the propeller shaft. Occasionally it is as well to take a look inside the gear-box to see how the teeth are getting on—once a year should be quite often enough and at the same time it is desirable to drain the old oil out to get rid of as many of the iron chippings as possible. If you are in any doubt as to the correct level to which the box should be filled, half-way up the lower shaft is plenty high enough. Most gear-boxes run happily on engine oil and absorb less power than with a thicker fluid. However, if it was originally intended that your box was to be grease lubricated you will be advised to see if it has any oil seals before making a change as, if it has none, you will soon be labelled as the man who always leaves a pool of oil behind on the front drive. Synchromesh boxes must be filled with the recommended oil or trouble will arise with the synchronising clutches. The same remark applies to epicyclic gear-boxes. We shall not go into the details of adjusting epicyclic gear-boxes as, although it is well within the scope of an amateur to effect these adjustments, it is essential that he should understand the working of the box before he starts using the spanners on it and we would take nearly a complete chapter to give this information in an understandable form. However, maintenance manuals are still available for the more popular makes of this type of gear-box.

While looking at your gear-box consider whether the lever is working with the least possible free movement. Floppy gear levers spoil the precision of good gear changing and can often be put right by a little judicious building-up of the worn parts.

Occasionally check the tightness of the bolts holding the couplings on either end of the propeller shaft. These have been known to come undone and if the front end drops onto the road you will perform a Boy-Scout-and-pole type of antic before coming to rest. If you have a torque tube enclosing your propeller shaft inspect for any play in the ball coupling at the back of the gear-box. Looseness here will give judder in the transmission when you let in the clutch and can generally be adjusted out by removing a shim. When the car has the back axle jacked up drive the propeller shaft and see that it is running true. If it is bent it will detract greatly from the smoothness of your car's performance.

The Chassis Frame

Because no part of the frame is a working part owners often take for granted that nothing can ever go wrong with it. While true up to a point it is advisable to make a specific inspection of the frame occasionally. Signs of rust working out at the intersections generally means that the rivets are coming loose and should be replaced by bolts and nuts.

When cleaning the car watch out for any cracks starting to appear, particularly near to spring hangers. To aid your inspection try to keep the inside of the frame under the floor boards as clean as you can and remember that while a small crack can often be welded up in position by a skilled welder, if the frame fractures right through the only way to make a respectable job is virtually to take the whole car to pieces. This will land you back at the beginning of Chapter II of our previous book and while it may lead to a complete restoration of your favourite motor-car it will certainly keep you off the road for quite a long time.

CHAPTER IV

MAINTENANCE OF THE ENGINE

We now come to that part of a motor-car on which most owners seem to lavish a large proportion of whatever time and effort they devote to looking after their vehicle. Let us say at once that when an engine is in really good order the less it is meddled with the better. Confine your attention to keeping it really clean and well lubricated and only doing other work when it is absolutely necessary. This particularly applies today with the much improved fuels and oils available and if modern valves and sparking plugs are being used your engine should run for many thousands of miles without the need of major maintenance work. The operative clause in the above is that the engine is in really good order, and there are no half-measures here. When the bearings get loose and rumbley, the compressions are poor or the water in the radiator boils when it should not, or when oil pours from every joint and there is water in the sump, then you need something more than just maintenance, in fact you require the complete overhaul as outlined in Chapter VII of our previous book.

If, however, you are pleased with the performance and all seems well in the engine-room the following should be of some help in keeping the power flowing for many a long mile.

Lubrication

Oil is the first essential to a long and happy life for any engine. Use the correct grade of lubricant, SAE 30 to SAE 40 should be plenty heavy enough. The use of heavier grades will only make starting more difficult especially in cold weather. Lighter oils can be tried and may prove satisfactory but you will probably get a big drop in oil pressure and you may also get excessive leaking from the shaft seals. Never use a detergent oil unless the engine has been completely stripped and thoroughly cleaned out.

If you should be suffering from a slipping clutch this may be due to oil leaking from the back main bearing and this complaint can sometimes be cured by using a heavier grade of oil in the engine. Such a remedy should only be considered as temporary and an effective repair of the offending bearing and seal ought to be carried out as soon as possible. Should the oil pressure be very low the trouble may only be due to dirt or fluff in the pressure relief valve but it could also be corrosion of the valve and seating, wear in the oil pump, wear in the bearings or even a faulty oil pressure gauge.

If you have any oil leaks try to cure them at once and any external oil pipes should be stripped down and thoroughly cleaned out occasionally. The oil filter should also be cleaned periodically, if it is solid with old gummy deposit have it degreased and then dipped in caustic soda solution as these deposits are very difficult to remove in any other way. The filters fitted to old engines are perfectly satisfactory if they are in good condition so there is no need to spoil the appearance of your engine by fitting a modern filter.

Drain the sump and refill with fresh oil every 3,000 miles. Always examine the old oil for metal particles as this will give you warning of impending trouble and may prevent a complete break-down at an inconvenient time.

The Cooling System

Always fill the radiator with soft water as the water passages are very small indeed and will soon become choked with lime deposit if you use hard water. If you do not live in a soft water area you should use rain water. Drain and flush out the system occasionally to prevent the build up of rust and dirt. If you suspect that the radiator is becoming choked you can carry out the test described in Chapter IX of our first book. Should this test show partial clogging of the radiator we would advise you to try one of the radiator-cleansing compounds, of which there are several on the market, before sending it to a repairer for what may be a somewhat expensive re-build. Inspect the radiator periodically for leaks but if these are present we do not advise the use of sealing compounds as they only make a very temporary repair and contribute to the choking up of the block; it is better to have the radiator re-conditioned by a reputable repairer.

On the radiator and also on the bulkhead of most cars there is a flange on to which the bonnet sits. The flange is fitted with a thick fabric strip known as bonnet tape which is threaded through slots in the flange and prevents a metal to metal contact between the bonnet and its supports which would otherwise cause rapid wear and noise. The tape is frequently in a very tatty state. There is no excuse for this as bonnet tape is readily obtainable from coachbuilders suppliers and is very easily fitted. Examine the hoses and if they show signs of decay replace them at once. If they look good externally but you know that they are very old it is advisable to replace them regardless of their appearance as sometimes the inside collapses while the outside still seems to be in good condition. You then get over-heating and the contretemps usually happens on a very hot day miles from any brook or service station.

The water jackets of all cast cylinder blocks have holes through which the cores were removed after casting and the arrangement for sealing these holes is often a source of leakage. There are three methods of sealing the core holes. The first is by a plate held on by a plurality of screws and if this is leaking the plate must be removed, the mating surfaces thoroughly cleaned, the plate planished and then refitted with a new gasket and sealing compound. The second type is the screwed plug but this pattern rarely leaks. If however it should the method of repair will be obvious. The last method is by a domed or Welch washer and since these are made of thin steel they are the most likely to give trouble. They can be bought in all the necessary sizes and the replacement is very easy. To remove a washer which is leaking, drill a hole about ¼ in. diameter near the centre and lever it out with a tommy bar taking care not to damage the rebate. To fit the new washer, place it in the rebate and then flatten the dome with a flat punch, the washer will be expanded into the rebate and a perfect joint achieved without any sealing compound (see fig. 4).

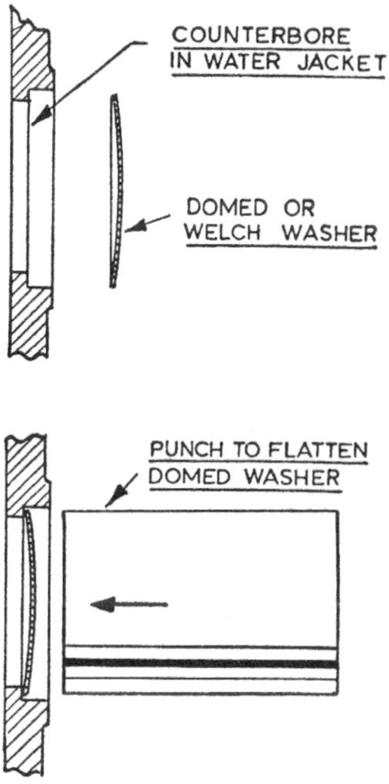

4 *Replacing a core plug*

The Water Pump

See that the bearing is lubricated regularly and always use H.M.P. water pump grease, but use this sparingly as any excess will find its way into the cooling system and eventually choke the radiator. Make sure that there is sufficient packing in the gland and that it is properly adjusted, but do not tighten it too much or you will absorb a vast amount of your valuable horse power. If you get persistent leaking at the gland it is probably due to a worn bearing, shaft, or both, and in this case it is useless to try to stop the leak by madly greasing, the only cure will be to have the pump reconditioned. If you are having this done it might be worth considering scrapping the gland which is rather a crude piece of construction and fitting a modern synthetic rubber oil-seal.

The Fan

Occasionally check the condition of the fan bearings and for this purpose you must first remove the belt. If the bearings are in a satisfactory state they should be lubricated with H.M.P. grease. Make sure that the belt is in good condition and that it is properly adjusted. If your fan has flat pulleys the best type of belt is one made of raw-hide and preferably endless with a cemented joint as any type of fastener would be very noisy. If you have vee pulleys, using either a Whittle or rubber belt, make certain that the belt or pulleys are not so worn that the belt is at the bottom of the groove as all the drive should be taken through the sides of the belt.

The Sparking Plugs and High Tension Leads

The sparking plug is probably one of the most neglected components in a motor-car. Its correct functioning however, is absolutely essential to the well-being of your engine and for its size it has an enormous amount of work to perform in very difficult conditions of heat and pressure. It will therefore well repay a certain amount of attention. It is essential that the plug is of the correct pattern for your engine. For instance, a hard plug in a cool engine would be prone to oiling up; a soft plug in a hot engine would be liable to cause pre-ignition and it would have a very short life. The reach of a plug, that is the length of the threaded portion, is also of great importance, as if you use one which is too long it may be struck by the piston with calamitous results. Examine your plugs every 3,000 miles, cleaning them thoroughly internally and externally with petrol and a stiff brush and setting the electrodes to the correct gap depending on the type of ignition, 0·019 in. for magneto and 0·025 in. for coil. If a plug is found to be faulty discard it at once, but in any case it is good practice to fit a new set of plugs every 10,000 miles. Cleanliness of the external surface of the plug insulator will certainly be a great help to easy starting.

A convenient method of testing whether or not a plug is sparking is first to have the engine running, then place a screwdriver with the end resting on the cylinder head and move the blade until it touches the plug terminal. If the engine slows down when the terminal is earthed then the plug is working, if the engine continues to run as before then the plug or its supply has failed.

Check your high tension leads. It is often observed when examining an otherwise well preserved motor-car that the engine is equipped with superbly decorative and highly polished metallic H.T. conduits which are filled with an incredibly sticky tangle of cables so full of points where a short can take place that the poor benighted spark must be rushing about like a wind in a colander. You should look for deterioration of the insulation due to oil, actual wearing through of the outer casing caused by abrasion, and breakage of the wire as the result of vibration. In making-up new leads we have found that the new plastic coated cable is very good as it is unaffected by hot oil and is so easy to keep clean. We will take the opportunity of pointing out that unless the entire ignition system is in first-class condition it is quite impossible to judge the remainder of the engine. Magnetos, coils and distributors will be fully dealt with in Chapter VII.

The Carburetter

It would not be possible to give the tuning instructions for all the different makes and types of carburetter as this would take up an entire book. We shall therefore confine our remarks to the most common faults and points which require regular service.

Clean the jets, passages and float chamber occasionally, and if you find an excessive amount of dirt it may indicate that your fuel system does not incorporate a filter or if it does that the gauze is damaged. When cleaning out fine jets do not blow through them with your mouth as your breath is liable to condense inside and form a beery globule which is just as bad as the dirt you wish to remove. Poking out with soft fine wire or blowing through with a tire pump are much more satisfactory methods. If your engine is fitted with an air filter make sure that you clean it every 5,000 miles otherwise if it gets thoroughly clogged up, it will cause a great drop in power. Examine the fuel pipe, the filter and also the vent hole in the petrol tank so that you can be sure that there is a continuous supply of fuel to the carburetter. While you are carrying out the examination be sure that the piping is in good condition and well supported to protect it against fracture due to vibration. See that the petrol pipe is well away from the exhaust system as proximity to this source of heat is liable to cause a vapour lock in hot weather resulting in the mysterious stoppage of the engine due to lack of petrol when everything seems to be in order. Other great sources of trouble are air leaks in the induction system. They may cause uneven running but, even worse, starting will be made difficult because of the weakening of the mixture. Points to check are: the throttle spindle bearings; the joints between the carburetter and the inlet manifold; between the manifold and the cylinder block; the piping and its unions connecting the inlet manifold to the autovac; suction screen-wipers or vacuum servo motor. Is the strangler or rich mixture device on the carburetter in working order? It must open and close properly. The throttle return spring must be in good condition and should be so fitted that the throttle would be closed if the linkage became detached. Flooding of the carburetter may be caused by an excessive accumulation of dirt in the float chamber fouling the needle valve seating, a bent or sticking needle valve or a punctured float which of course will sink and allow the valve to remain open after the float chamber has filled. It is sound practice to empty the petrol tank completely very occasionally to get rid of any water or dirt which may have accumulated. Examine the fibre washers on the joints and petrol unions and see that they are not leaking. On a car fitted with an S.U. instrument examine the jet gland, and should it be leaking it must be re-corked, but if you have to do this make sure that you centre the jet with its needle upon reassembly. This type of carburetter is fitted with a dashpot, the spindle of which must be kept lubricated with thin oil. This piston must not be oiled but it should be kept clean.

The Autovac

This instrument is incredibly reliable and seems to last for ever, so if your car is fitted with one you should have very little trouble. However, if any faults do occur the makers will overhaul it for you. The only attention required is to see that each union is making a sound joint and periodically to drain off any water or dirt via the small drain tap provided.

The Electric Fuel Pump

Keep the filter clean and see that there is no dirt on the disc valves. Occasionally clean up the contact points. To test the pump disconnect the pipe from the outlet and then switch on; the pump should run quickly and if it does not do this then you are going to be short of fuel at full throttle. To carry out this test you will need to fit a rubber pipe on to the outlet of the pump so that the flow of petrol can be collected in some suitable vessel. If your pump should prove to be unsatisfactory the best proposition is to fit a reconditioned unit unless you have one of the rare and obsolete models in which case you will either have to overhaul it yourself or fit a modern S.U. pump.

The Mechanical Fuel Pump

Clean the filter and when you are refitting it make sure that the bowl is seating properly on its washer, as if you have any leaks here you will find that the pump sucks air instead of petrol. Keep the valves clean and the unions tight and make sure that the operating arm has not worn and so reduced the stroke of the pump. To test, remove both inlet and outlet pipes and detach the pump from the engine, the arm operating the diaphragm can then be worked by hand. Place your thumb over the outlet port having depressed the operating arm, when the arm should not return until your thumb is removed. If the arm does return then either one or other of the valves are leaking or the diaphragm is fractured, which can be ascertained by stripping and inspection.

The Air Compressor and Pressure System

Certain cars are fitted with an engine-driven air compressor for pressurising the fuel system and such pumps require very little maintenance. See that the valves are clean and seating properly and add a few drops of engine oil occasionally if the pump is fitted with an oil cup. The pump should not deliver air at a pressure of more than 2–3 lb. per sq. in. as this is as high a pressure as the fuel tank will stand.

The Supercharger

A supercharger may be lubricated by oil which has either been mixed with the petrol or piped to the bearings from the engine. In any case it will certainly require oil, so make sure that it is getting there in the correct quantity. If blow-off valves are fitted keep them clean and in order but do not alter the pressure settings. Check that the blower is giving its rated pressure—if there is no pressure gauge fitted you will have to connect one to some part of the induction system between the blower and the engine to carry out this test. Remember that the blower can only give its rated pressure at full revs and when the engine is under full load, i.e. on the road while pulling the car along at full throttle opening. If the blower is worn out, that is if it is not giving somewhere near the correct pressure, it will be adding little or nothing to the power of the engine but at the same time it will be absorbing quite a lot of power from the engine. In such a case you may be better off to discard it and to fit a plain induction system if repair of the blower is out of the question. An alternative would be to fit a suitable current production blower which would probably be cheaper than to have the old one reconditioned.

A word of warning: since the carburetter is bolted direct on to the supercharger its position will probably be fairly low down, and in this case take care not to drive the car through deep water. The water would be sucked in causing an hydraulic lock and the probable wrecking of your engine.

Decarbonising

The combustion of the mixture causes carbon to be deposited within the cylinder head and, since carbon is a very poor conductor of heat when it is present in very large quantities, it causes overheating, pinking and loss of power. Some of the carbon may even become incandescent and it will then cause pre-ignition. The mileage after which an engine will need decarbonising will vary with the design of engine, the amount of wear in the bores and pistons and the quality of the oil and fuel used. It may be anything between 10,000 and 20,000 miles or it can be left longer if you are satisfied with the performance. There is nothing to be gained by decarbonising before it is necessary, unless the valves need attention, as these two jobs will invariably be done at the same time. It is very necessary that the valves are kept in good condition otherwise the performance is bound to be poor and starting may be extremely difficult due to the lack of compression. The test for this is to turn the engine over slowly by hand with the starting handle, observing if all the compressions are there and if they are good enough. Of course, poor compressions could be caused by badly worn pistons and bores or by broken piston rings, but these would also be shown up by excessive oil consumption. If your engine is an early side valve type with valve caps you will be able to clean and grind in the valves without disturbing any other part of the engine. If, however, the engine has a detachable head this will have to be removed or if it has a fixed head then the entire cylinder block will have to come off for both valve grinding and decarbonising. The removal of a cylinder head is usually more easy if the engine is warm, tapping round the outer edge with a mallet after the nuts have been removed will help to loosen the joint. Try also turning the engine with the starter when the compressions will force up the head and you should be able to lift it off quite easily. There are usually several points from which it is possible to lever off the head but take care not to damage the joint faces.

If your engine is of the overhead camshaft type take a note of the timing marks before you strip down the drive. To remove the carbon you can

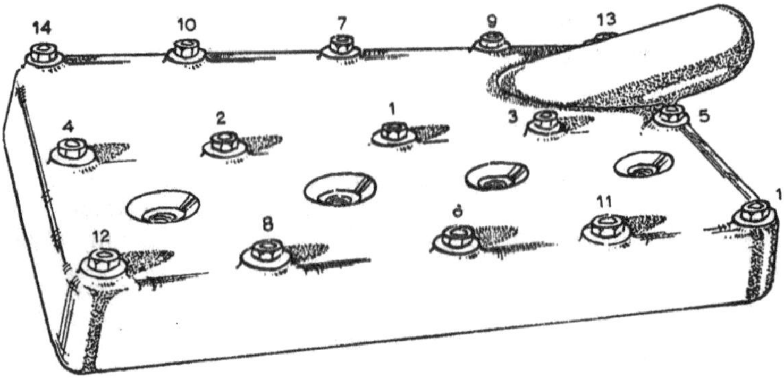

5 *Correct sequence for tightening a multiplicity of nuts to avoid distortion*

use scrapers, not too sharp for aluminium pistons and heads, or better still rotary wire brushes in an electric drill. If the bores are worn leave a ring of carbon round the outside edge of the piston crown as this helps to act as an oil seal and you will otherwise have an even heavier oil consumption than you had before. Before cleaning the carbon from the cylinder block and pistons, in the case of a detachable head, it is advisable to close with rag all the water passages and also the bores other than the ones on which you are working. For further details see Chapter VII in our previous book.

When removing or replacing cylinder heads always loosen or tighten the nuts a little at a time and in the order shown in fig. 5. This is to prevent distortion of the cylinder head casting and consequential perviousness of the joint with the cylinder block. Always use a new gasket if possible and when fitting the gasket paint it over both sides with a thin coat of "Payenite" or gold size. Whenever possible the raised edges of a copper asbestos gasket should be placed against the cylinder block. After the car has run 100–200 miles the nuts should again be tightened.

The Tappets

Keep the tappets adjusted always setting them to the clearance specified by the manufacturer. Do not imagine that by reducing the clearance from standard you will make the valve gear quieter. It will be just as noisy and you will have altered the valve timing which may be to the detriment of the engine's performance. Worst of all you will have made the dreaded burning of the valves more likely. If you have one of those rare engines for which there are no instructions in existence and therefore you do not know the correct tappet clearances then we suggest that you set them all at 0·010 in. Having set them to this dimension when the engine is cold check them again when it is hot and if the gap has closed you must open it back to 0·010 in. This may not give you quite the correct timing but at least you should be safe. See that the valves are quite free and not sticking and that the springs are in good condition.

The Controls

It is worth while spending a little time and effort on the controls and their linkage so that they work with Rolls-Royce precision and smoothness.

Keep all the joints and bearings well lubricated and adjust them so as to eliminate all lost motion and rattles. Make sure that movement of the operating lever of every control is producing the full required movement at the other end, such as movement from full advance to full retard at the distributor. Have only the minimum tension on any return springs, provided that there is sufficient tension for safety, as in the case of the accelerator in particular a heavy spring makes driving very tiring.

The Exhaust System

Examine all the joints for leaks and occasionally tighten the manifold nuts. Keep the system underneath the car well painted with heat-resisting paint. It makes a very nice clean job if you have your exhaust manifold aluminiumised. This finish completely cures all the rusting troubles and you might also consider the same treatment for the silencer and exhaust piping, in which case you will still need to paint the part under the car as the aluminium, being white, will look very flashy. A very good paint for this purpose is "Kemick" heat-resisting black made by I.C.I. Ltd. This must be applied in two coats, and between applications the metal must be heated in order that the proper chemical action may take place. Remember that when you have had any steel parts aluminiumised they cannot be welded, as the aluminium alloys with the steel. If you need to fit new jointing washers they should be copper-asbestos or copper for the manifold, and further back Walkerite or similar material will be satisfactory.

The Clutch

Whatever type of clutch is fitted to your car make sure that it is adjusted to give complete withdrawal and also to give clearance at the thrust bearing. Ascertain that this race is kept lubricated with H.M.P. grease.

Cone clutches lined with "Ferodo" need no special attention, but if the lining is leather it should be dressed periodically with collan oil or neats-foot oil and if it is a cotton lining anoint it with engine oil. After dressing, the clutch should be left propped out overnight. When dry plate clutches are properly adjusted they need no attention but some multi-plate metal-to-metal clutches are lubricated with flake graphite and others need oil, cork insert clutches also run in oil but this is usually fed from the engine.

If your leather cone clutch suffers from slipping the cure is to dress it with Fuller's earth. If a dry plate clutch slips it may be caused by oil on the lining and you could possibly cure this by spraying it with a carbon tetrachloride fire extinguisher. A permanent cure is to remove the plate and have it degreased. Slipping could also be caused by weak springs or jamming of the centre plate on its splines but to check this you will have to strip the clutch. All clutches of the lined variety should be relined when they are down to the rivets.

The only attention required by a fluid flywheel is topping up with the correct grade of oil.

CHAPTER V

MAINTENANCE OF THE BODYWORK INTERIOR

BEFORE we start on the serious business of discussing details under the above heading we would like to stress that we have now come to that part of the car where it is possible to enlist the aid of any member of the female sex who happens to be around and who can be persuaded that she has nothing better to do. Much of the work is so closely allied to the maintenance of the drawing room that not only will you find a hidden wealth of inborn skill in the lady's fingers but also will you find that women in general have a great deal more patience than men in this sort of work, particularly if the men are like us who are keener on the engineering than on the soft furnishings.

Upholstery and Seats

It is very much more easy to tackle the cleaning of the car furniture outside the car itself and by getting the various pieces out into the daylight you are less likely to miss those defects which you have got so used to looking at in their normal positions. At regular intervals therefore, take out all the detachable seats and squabs and give them a good cleaning. The upholstery that is more firmly attached to the bodywork will obviously have to be worked on *in situ* but this is more easily done if you have made room for yourself by taking out of the car as much as possible.

Your car may have leather upholstery and this is usually motor hide, that is a leather with a doped finish. The best method of cleaning such leather is to use soap and warm water with either a cloth or a soft scrubbing brush. Before starting with the water it is as well to brush out as much as possible of the dust and fluff from the pleats, removing only the ingrained dirt and grease with the soap and water. Never use any hydrocarbons to clean leather as these will permanently damage the surface. If your upholstery leather is brown it may be furniture hide, which was used in certain luxury cars, and this has no doped finish and must not be washed as it absorbs water very quickly. You can test whether your leather is of this variety by applying a damp cloth to it and seeing whether the dampness is absorbed or remains on the surface. Should you have furniture hide it must be treated, after removing as much dirt as possible using a slightly damp cloth, with Connolly's "C.B. Hide Food". The more normal motor hide benefits greatly from a treatment with this preparation after washing provided that it has been allowed to become thoroughly dry first.

Some lower-priced cars were upholstered in leather cloth and here again soap, warm water and elbow grease are the best cleaning agents. After cleaning, a good polish with a soft dry rag should bring up the original finish. On no account use any form of polish on leather cloth as it will probably react with the surface making it sticky, particularly on warm days, and disastrous adhesions between passenger's clothing and the seat may result.

Another type of upholstery material is Bedford Cord. This is, of course, a textile material and can be cleaned in any way that you might clean a suit of clothes. A good vacuuming is essential before tackling any grease spots or other blemishes and this can be supplemented by brushing with a stiff brush particularly in any pleats or folds. Having removed all the dust use a dry cleaning liquid such as "Thawpit", working to the instructions on the bottle. On no account try to wash Bedford Cord as the water will go straight through and will take a very long time to dry out. When performing cleaning operations on any material of the plush variety always rub only in the direction of the pile, as otherwise the appearance will be spoilt. Pile that has become flattened due to long use can be raised by holding it in a jet of steam and this treatment will greatly improve the appearance of otherwise rather dowdy upholstery.

When you have attended to the main upholstery you will, of course, finish by giving the same treatment to the inside of the doors and any other parts of the interior which are finished with the same material. If there are defects which cleaning will not bring back to a good condition you will find further instructions for repair and restoration in our previous book.

While adjustable front seats are out of the car clean and lightly oil the seat runners and the adjustment mechanism. When you are doing this see that the runners are properly anchored to the floor and that the seats themselves are in good condition. One is often asked to try what is otherwise a very pleasant looking car only to find on taking one's place behind the wheel that the driver's seat is in the last stages of disintegration, being apparently held in place largely by faith, with the back rest floating about between the limits of the side of the car and passenger's seat, the seat cushion at least three inches lower than original and generally a misery. It is essential for the full enjoyment of driving any car to have a comfortable and stable seat which holds you in exactly the right position and which allows you to use the wheel only for steering and not as an anchor. You will find it worth while to experiment with a few loose cushions both underneath and behind you to see if your seat is still really in the right position vertically and horizontally. The rake of the seat-back is very critical and having ascertained exactly what suits you best it is worth going to some trouble, and expense if necessary, to get the driving seat into that position.

Before passing onto the next section may we also say that we hope you will never resort to loose covers on your upholstery. Seats that are obviously worn with long service but that have the appearance of having regular care, look far more in keeping with a Vintage car than natty chintz covers run up by Aunt Fanny.

Carpets and Floors

The best maintenance for carpets is regular vacuum cleaning. Nothing wears a carpet out faster than leaving grit between the pile and with this small attention a good carpet will last a very long time. However, it is beneficial to take the carpets out from time to time and to give them a good beating as even a vacuum cleaner does not seem to remove all the grit. While they are out examine them for oil and tar stains which can be removed with petrol or "Thawpit". An excellent preparation for getting your carpets as clean as possible is "1001 Carpet Cleaner" which has full instructions for use on the bottle.

If your carpets have nothing between them and the floorboards you would be well advised to consider fitting underfelt or, better still, the modern rubber underlay which is completely waterproof. Either of these will greatly increase the length of life of your carpets and also give a much more luxurious feel underfoot. Another benefit of a thicker floor covering is better insulation from both heat and noise coming up through the floor, and most Vintage cars can well do with as much as you can give them in this respect. Another touch of luxury worth considering is to bind the edges of the carpets with leather or P.V.C. cloth to match the upholstery if they are not already so treated and this is the sort of job that can easily be done a little at a time without interfering with the normal use of your car.

There are generally signs of heavy wear on the driver's side of the front carpet and although the usual repair is to rivet or stitch a patch of ribbed rubber matting or leather over this area, an alternative is to have made a fitted coco-nut mat, of the front porch variety, if the position of the pedals will allow this which is merely put on top of the carpet and is rigid enough to hold itself in place. The Birmingham Institute for the Blind can supply such a mat made to a paper template.

The floorboards on early Vintage cars were sometimes covered with linoleum or rubber. Either of these benefit from a scrub with soap and water followed by a polish with furniture polish for the linoleum or black boot polish for the rubber. Ribbed aluminium floor coverings are best treated with a wire brush or wire wool working in the direction of the grooves.

The next time that you remove your floorboards for chassis maintenance it will probably come as a shock to you, if you spend a little time looking at them, to see what a state they are in. First thoroughly clean the under-

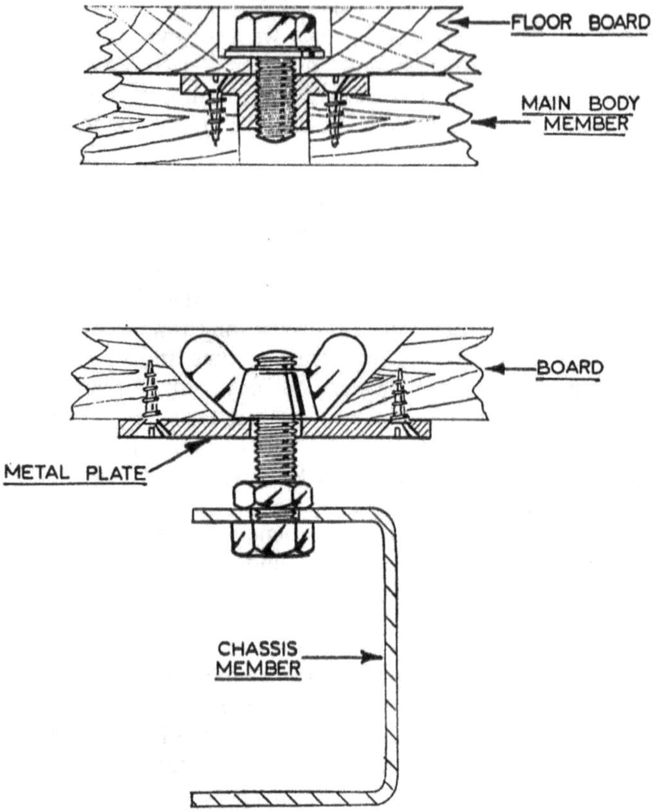

6 *Methods of fixing floorboards*

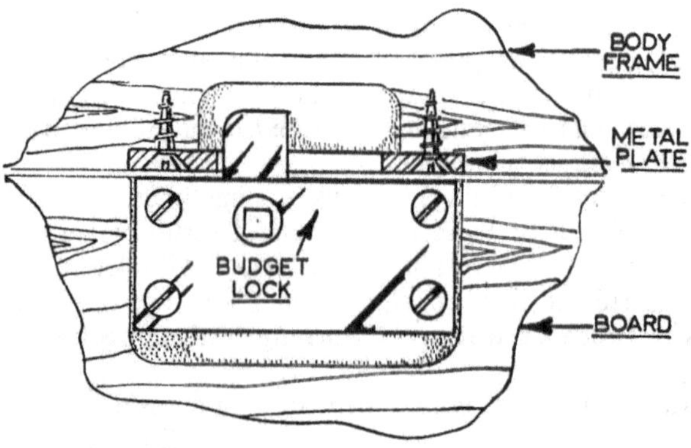

side. This is generally very oily and takes a considerable amount of petrol and time to get clean. If they were painted with a glossy paint they could be kept clean very much more easily and this would also preserve the wood. An early form of heat and noise insulation practised by certain Vintage constructors was to glue a thick layer of felt on the underside of all the floorboards. This gets into the most horrible state, but because it is out of sight for most of the time it is ignored. When you next have the time you might consider tearing off the old felt and replacing it with new felt but adding a cover of sheet aluminium over the felt which is very easy to clean and also tends to reflect heat rising from beneath and so adds to the insulation.

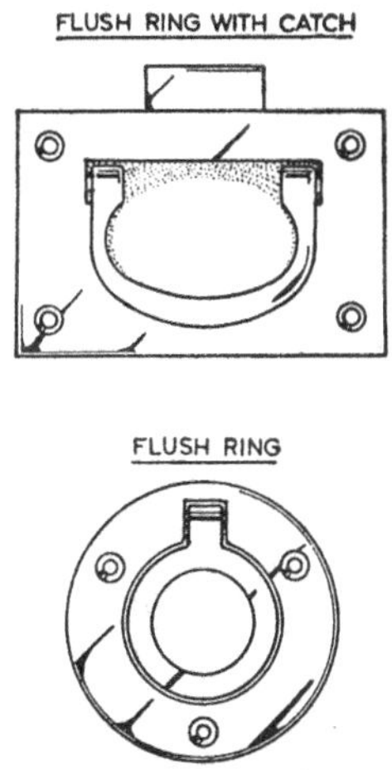

7 *Floorboard lifting rings*

Another prevalent source of trouble is the method of securing the boards. In certain cars they are held down merely by wood-screws into the lower body members. These inevitably strip their threads and a stage is often reached where the boards are not really held in place by anything but their own weight. There is quite a variety of methods of making a good job of the floorboard fixings. One is to insert tapped metal sockets into the body frame where the old screws used to fit and to use metal threaded set-screws to engage with these. Another solution is to fit vertical threaded studs onto suitable chassis cross-members with corresponding holes in the boards, the clamping being done with wing nuts recessed into the boards. A third idea is to fit budget locks, obtainable from coachbuilders' suppliers, into the edges of the boards and engaging with sockets in the main body frame. These three alternatives are shown in fig. 6. In order to avoid having to prise up the boards with a screwdriver you can fit flush-ring floorboard lifts, also still available from coachbuilders' suppliers. (see fig. 7.)

Any replacement floorboards should be made from resin-bonded plywood of the requisite thickness as it is far stronger and less likely to warp than a single plank. Always paint them well with several coats of paint to keep out damp and rot.

The Headlining

The headlining of most Vintage saloon cars, if it is the original, has generally by now got into rather a bad state. By the very nature of the material it tends to gather dust and grime very easily and it gradually seems to absorb the tar from cigarette smoke until it assumes a brown tinge and gives off a nasty odour which no amount of ventilation will disperse. If the headlining in your car is still taut and has suffered no actual damage you can make quite a good job of cleaning it by going over the whole surface a little at a time with a dry cleaner like "Thawpit". Although the job takes quite a considerable time and is rather akin to Michael Angelo painting the roof of St. Peter's, you will be pleasantly surprised when you have finished by how much the inside of the car is lightened and how fresh the air smells when next you use the car. If the headlining has gone loose and baggy there is little that you can do but to replace it as described in our previous book. Headlining material is relatively so cheap compared with the cost or labour of fitting that it is not worth putting back the old fabric if for any reason it has to be removed.

Doors and Door Furniture

It goes without saying that in the routine maintenance of your car you will apply a drop of oil to the hinges and bolts of your doors but the time inevitably arrives when a little more than this is necessary to keep everything working smoothly. With the door open try lifting it up and down to check the play in the hinges. You will probably find that there is considerable shake and to rectify this you will have to remove the hinges from both door and door pillar. You can either remove the hinge pins first and then unscrew the hinges from the woodwork, or the reverse, whichever is the more convenient. Mark the components before removing. You can then either replace the hinges with new ones or drill out the hinge pin holes to an oversize and make up new and larger pins. The latter is generally the best method as new hinges will come to you undrilled for their fastening screws and you will have to be very careful indeed to get the door back to its original position. Stainless steel makes an ideal pin as most of the wear which takes place in hinges is due to corrosion of the normal mild steel pins. When performing the drilling operation on the hinge pin holes you must drill both halves of the hinge in one operation or the holes will not line up.

Very often the wood-screws that secure the hinges have stripped their threads in the wood. If this is so and the wood is still sound a perfect repair can be made by inserting a Rawlplug in the hole, which has been drilled out to the correct size, before replacing the screw. Always use new screws if the old ones are rusty as these will tear the wood and soon come loose again. It is a good idea to oil all wood-screws before use. If the timber has become rotten where the hinge is fitted it is sometimes possible to cut away the bad wood and to insert a panel of new hardwood, preferably ash, gluing it in place with "Casco" or a similar modern adhesive.

While attending to the hinges see if the bolt of the door lock is still engaging with its striker plate in the correct position or if the door is rubbing on its bottom edge. Incorrect door positioning can sometimes be rectified by packing out either the upper or lower hinge, depending on the direction in which the door is misplaced.

Now turn your attention to the door lock. With the door closed test for free movement between the bolt and the striker plate. Play can sometimes be adjusted out by moving the striker plate if such an adjustment is provided on your car. On the older type of car there is often no adjustment as the striker plate is held in place with two wood-screws. On no account try moving the wood-screws to a new position as the new holes will be so near to the original ones that the screws will soon become loose. The cure is either to build up the striker plate by soldering on a new piece of metal as shown in fig. 8 or to fit a new plate. It may be that the rubber door stops have worn to a point where their replacement will take all the play out of the bolt. Most shapes of door stops are still available from coachbuilders' suppliers but if yours should be unfortunately unavailable it is not too difficult to cut new ones from a block of rubber. The wedge-action metal door stops fitted to the later pre-war cars are still available and a considerable improvement in the door fastening can often be obtained by their replacement. These also require light oiling together with the locks and hinges.

8 *Repairing a striker plate*

Turning now to the lock itself, examine the bolt—particularly for its fit in the body of the lock. The rectangular hole through which it passes is often badly worn and is a common source of door rattle. Here again it is possible to remove the lock and to insert by brazing a piece of new metal to bring the lock body back to its original size.

Most of the older patterns of lock and door handles are now extremely difficult to replace as stocks have disappeared, but John Aronson Limited give a service of repair to most patterns and will also repair window regulators if they are not too far decayed. There are certain door handles still on the market which do not look out of keeping on a Vintage car and if you are in need of a replacement it will probably be necessary to fit a complete set in order that all the handles match. If your door handles merely need replating then of course this can easily be done, but if they are made of zinc alloy you will have to take them to an electro-plater who has the necessary equipment to deal with this material as it cannot be plated by the same process as other metals.

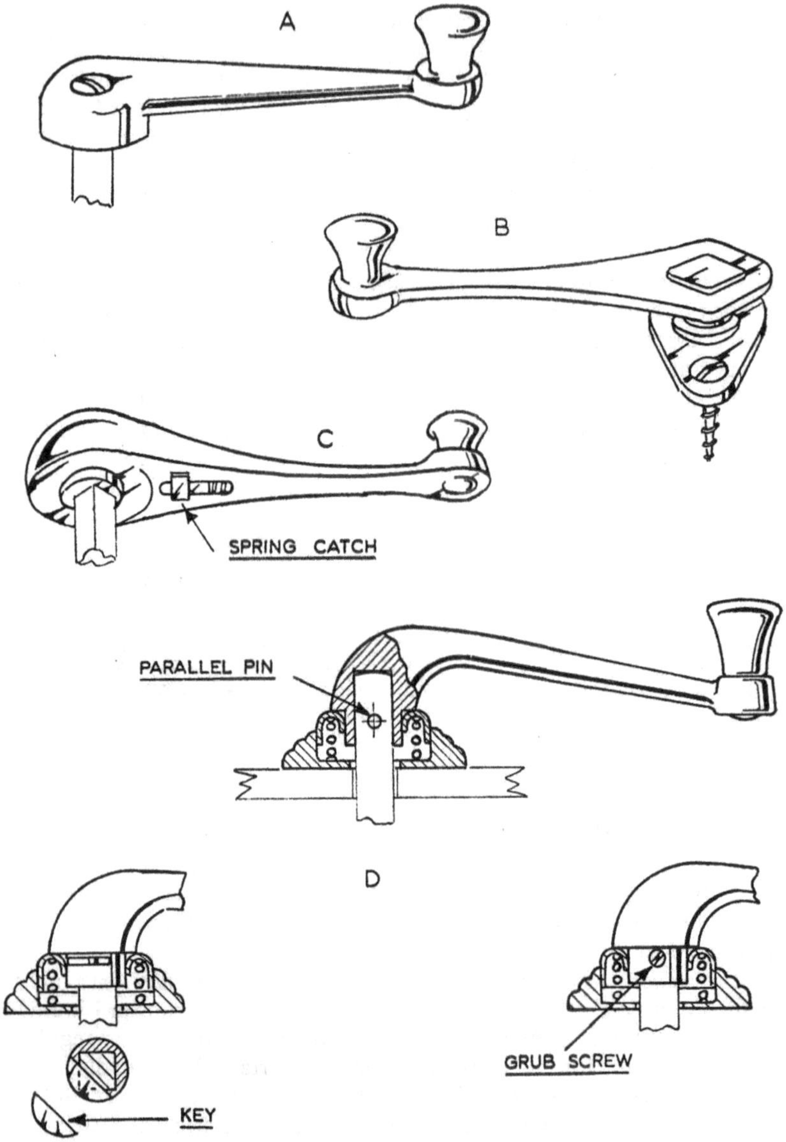

9 *Methods of fastening inner lock and window regulator handles*

It is a good idea occasionally to take the inner linings off the doors and to investigate the condition of both the lock mechanism and the window regulators as these generally get into a fair state of corrosion and decay being out of sight. To do this you will have to remove the inner door handle and the window regulator handle. These are held on by a variety of fastenings, some of which are not at all obvious, but if you refer to fig. 9 you will doubtless find your type of handle. To remove A or B it is only necessary to take out the screws, type C has a spring loaded catch behind the handle and to remove this type the catch should be pulled outwards from the spindle when the handle will be released. Type D has a spring loaded escutcheon plate and this must first be pushed back from the handle when the fixing will be disclosed and may be either a parallel pin, a small key or a grub screw. The window regulator mechanism is generally very reliable but can do with an occasional cleaning and oiling. Particularly note the condition of the channel into which the glass is secured to the regulator. Because of rain running down the window the channel often slowly rusts away and finally the glass becomes detached. It is not too difficult to make up a new channel or to send the whole regulator away to John Aronson Limited for repair. The glass is generally held in purely by being a force fit into the rubber lined channel. At the bottom of the doors of all closed cars there are one or more holes so that any water that runs in down the glass can drain out, these holes tend to get clogged up with a mixture of fluff and dirt and should be cleaned out regularly.

Look at the door check-straps. They have usually stretched with long usage and new ones are easily made either from leather or balata belting covered with upholstery material. Stitching of these straps can generally be done by the local shoe repairer or you can, of course, hand stitch them. The screws which hold the straps to the woodwork of the body have a very hard time and are worth looking at and replacing if they are bent or loose. The metal staples or slides which are used with certain types of check-strap are still available from coachbuilders' suppliers but send a pattern as there are many different designs.

Finally, have a look at the channels in which the windows run, which are made from velvet-covered rubber, and the weather-strip made from similar material which seals the bottom of the window. If the windows rattle then it shows that these two items are in need of replacement. Both are available from coachbuilders' suppliers but it is important to state the thickness of the glass when ordering the channel as there are various sizes.

The window regulators in partition windows between the front and rear compartments of limousines work on the same principle as the door windows and must receive the same maintenance. In a late pre-war car fitted with an electric-motor driven partition if the mechanism is faulty and beyond repair a modern replacement can be supplied for the whole mechanism by the Piper Electric Blind and Window Operator Co. Limited as most of the original electric regulators are now not repairable by the makers.

Windscreens, Windows and Sidescreens

Turning now to the actual glass in your car this must by law be of safety glass in the windscreen. In our experience we still come across Vintage car owners driving round behind plate glass screens quite unaware of the fact, and if you acquire an original-looking car it is well worth the trouble to make quite sure that it has safety glass fitted before going on the road, as if you have an accident involving someone getting injured by a plate glass screen your insurance will not cover you for any damages. Of the two types of safety glass available we much prefer the laminated for windscreens having experienced the sudden blackout when a toughened screen disintegrates, but this is a matter that only you can decide. Toughened glass is much cheaper than laminated. There is no legal necessity to fit safety glass in the side windows but if you have to replace any of them obviously you will fit the safer material. Winding windows are less likely to crack if made from toughened glass and as a sudden change from transparent to opaque does not matter in a side window we would advise its use in this position.

The rubber seals round moveable windscreens gradually harden and perish and most rubber sections are still available from coachbuilders' suppliers. Nothing is more annoying than to have water running down the inside of your screen when driving in the rain and this can generally be cured by replacement of the sealing strips.

Many pre-war cars were fitted with opening windscreens or screens which were divided up into sections, some of which were moveable. All these are likely sources of trouble and we will go so far as to say that if it does not change the appearance of your car too much you will be well advised to consider fitting a single piece of glass to the whole screen. In the case of a Vee screen, which must be retained to keep the character of the coachwork, then it may be possible to reduce the number of pieces of glass to two. On an open car with a folding screen make sure that the seal between the body and the screen, or the two parts of the screen, is in good order; certain original designs can be greatly improved upon at this point by the use of a different section of sealing strip of which there is a great variety.

Open cars usually rely on the windscreen frame for the front anchorage of the hood which puts a considerable stress on the frame itself. See that the screen is anchored to the body securely, particularly if this is achieved by the use of woodscrews. They could probably be replaced by metal screws passing right through the woodwork and fitted with large washers and nuts.

On open cars the celluloid in the side curtains has often become fairly opaque with age. A smooth surface can be regained by polishing with metal polish and, in very bad cases, this can be preceded by the use of cellulose cutting paste. Use a very soft duster for the final polishing. If the celluloid is broken then it will have to be replaced, and it is best to use "Vybac" for this purpose which is both more flexible and more durable than celluloid. The fabric parts of side curtains can be kept smart by brushing with a clothes brush but if they become stained a certain amount of cleaning can be achieved by rubbing with new bread.

Decorative Woodwork

The interior panelling, fillets, instrument panel and other decorative woodwork can be cleaned with soap and a damp cloth, afterwards finishing with a wax or furniture polish. If the surface is beyond restoring by mere polishing then the piece of wood must be removed from the car and inspected to see whether it is solid hardwood or only veneer. In the case of solid hardwood the normal process of sanding out the blemishes and putting on a new polish can be embarked upon as described in our previous book, but if the article has a veneer surface great care must be exercised. If the damage merely consists of the polish having gone the surface may be very carefully sanded with the finest garnet paper preparatory to re-polishing. Remember that the veneer is only paper thickness and if you rub through it the piece will have to be re-veneered. It often happens in drophead coupés that veneered wood has been subject to exposure and the veneer has lifted and broken off in certain places. It is possible for an amateur to cut back the veneer to a place where it is good and to glue a new matching piece, to sand the surface level and to repolish the whole. When glueing in a new piece of veneer, hold it in place with a clamp until the glue is perfectly set. Small quantities of various veneers are obtainable from Midland Veneers Service Co. Limited or if you know a local cabinet maker he will probably do the job for you better than you will ever do it yourself.

If you have any unwanted holes in your instrument panel and you are restoring its surface finish take the opportunity of filling them up with a plug of wood matching the original before doing the repolishing.

Most decorative woodwork is held in place with visible wood-screws which are nickel or chromium plated. A considerable smartening effect can be achieved by taking out all the screws and having them replated together with their cup washers. New screws and washers are available both plated or in stainless steel which are nearly as cheap as having the old screws replated.

Other Interior Accessories

Before leaving the interior of the bodywork have a look round at the minor accessories which adorn the inside of many cars. It is quite a simple matter to detach such items as ashtrays, interior door handles and light fittings and to restore them to their original condition without taking the car off the road to do so. It is surprising what a difference having a few such parts replated will do to cheer up the interior coachwork. Scuttle ventilators which no longer shut properly can generally still be replaced by new items of identical design still used in motor-coaches. Those strange devices known as pulls are often rather moth eaten and are still available from coachbuilders' suppliers. A flyblown rear-view mirror can easily be resilvered by the local household mirror expert. It is the attention to all these little details that makes the difference between a very ordinary motor-car and a really well turned out carriage.

All motor body fittings, accessories and trimming materials can be supplied by Albert Jagger Limited, but they may not be able to match your pattern and in this case you will have to use the nearest modern equivalent.

CHAPTER VI

MAINTENANCE OF THE BODYWORK EXTERIOR

SOME of the notes in this chapter may seem to go a little beyond the bounds of the word "maintenance" but as we are assuming that this book will be read in conjunction with our previous work, where the description of certain major repairs had to be omitted for reasons of space, we have included them here in the hope that they may be of use to at least a few enthusiasts in distress. We would like again to stress our great belief in retaining the original shape and appearance of your car. Very many Vintage and Thoroughbred motor-cars have had their bodywork chopped about unmercifully in the past twenty years, and whereas the owners no doubt derived a great deal of enjoyment at the time out of the resultant vehicle, the car was made quite valueless as a collector's piece. It therefore pays to see that the original bodywork or its replica is preserved to the limit of your ability.

Cleaning the Exterior of the Car

To maintain a car in good condition it must be cleaned regularly. We realise that this undertaking is a little inconvenient if you do not possess the necessary slaves but, in fact, the car should be washed as soon as it returns from any journey taken in bad weather, before the mud has had a chance to become dry. Apart from the slave or yourself who will provide the manpower, you will require a bucket, chamois leather and a sponge, either synthetic or the natural variety, and if possible a water supply and a hose not less than 25 ft. in length. You should also have a wheel brush which is an absolute necessity if your car is fitted with wire wheels. If possible a separate sponge and chamois leather should be kept for the chassis and the inside of the wings; this is to prevent any oil or grease that may be picked up when cleaning these parts of the car being transferred to the bodywork.

Before starting to wash the car all the windows, the windscreen and any ventilators should be shut. The engine may also be covered with a waterproof sheet inside the bonnet which, of course, should be closed. If the car is an open tourer the hood should be erected. The wheels should be jacked up clear of the ground so that they may be thoroughly cleaned; this will also enable the front wheels to be turned onto full lock and the cleaning of the front axle, springs and shock absorbers will be made more convenient thereby.

The principle to be followed in washing a car is to soften the mud by a good soaking so that the grit floats off and scratching of the paintwork is avoided. Therefore, when using the hose on the bodywork apply plenty of water at a low pressure until the entire area is well wetted. The pressure can be increased slightly to remove the softened mud and finally the sponge should be used to remove the last traces of dirt. Remember that the sponge is collecting grit from the panels so that it should be washed out repeatedly in the bucket. To prevent water getting inside the car do not direct the jet of water from the hose on to the edges of the doors, windows or ventilators or on to that side of the bonnet louvres which are open. When the bodywork is quite clean the water should be removed with the sponge and the panels can then be dried off with the chamois leather. Before the sponge and the leather are used for drying the car they must have been soaked in water and well squeezed out. If your car has a coach-painted finish the maximum care must be exercised while washing it as in the case of this finish even small scratches cannot be polished out. Cellulose paintwork and fabric covered bodies do not require quite so much care as the finish is less liable to suffer from the abrasion of the grit and small scratches in cellulose paintwork can be polished out.

A useful fitting for the hose is the Flexy washer, shown in fig. 10. This is a very soft brush with a rubber back which is screwed on to the end of the hose, the water passes through holes at the base of the bristles. This accessory can also be supplied with a container to hold detergent tablets which fits between the hose and the brush so that the car is then washed with a detergent foam. If, however, you do not wish to go to the expense of such equipment it is quite a good practice to put a little detergent in the bucket of water for the final spongeing of the body. Also in cold weather it is quite a good idea to have warm water in the bucket as not only will this be slightly more effective in removing any grease film but it also makes a rather dreary job somewhat more agreeable.

10 *The Flexy washer*

Fabric bodies which have become very grimy are a little difficult to clean and the only safe cleaning process that we can suggest is to give them a light scrubbing with a soft nail-brush in soap and water, but this should only be necessary on very infrequent occasions.

For washing the chassis and axles, the underside of the wings and the wheels a greater pressure of water from the hose may be used otherwise the treatment is the same as for the body. You will probably find that the wheel brush is useful for some of the more difficult chassis parts in addition to the wheels. There is always a fair amount of oil to be found on the chassis and on the axles round the spring shackles and steering joints and this can usually be removed with petrol or paraffin but if there is a very thick layer of oily mud you should use "Gunk". This is a preparation which renders oil and grease soluble in water and it should be painted on the ancient incrustations of greasy mud before the application of the hose.

Now that you have the car absolutely clean and ready for polishing make sure that it is really dry before you start on the next stage otherwise you will be plagued by small quantities of water emanating from corners and small crevices and causing a smear usually just as you have finished polishing a panel.

There are a number of makes of polish for the bodywork but whatever it says on the tin of your favourite brand the contents are only an aid to the job, ninety per cent of a really high gloss is muscular effort and so the rule is a very little polish and a lot of hard work.

Coachpaint must always be cleaned with water and polished with a good wax polish such as Johnson's Wax or Simoniz. Never use a cleaner or cutting compound however mild its action. When the surface has become too dull to be polished with wax and should the paintwork be still sound, then the only way to restore the finish is to rub it down with fine wet or dry paper and water and to give it one or two coats of varnish as described in our earlier book.

Cellulose paintwork is also much better if polished with wax as this not only gives it a high gloss but also adds to it a protective coating. This type of paint has the great advantage that dirt, stains and small scratches can be removed by preparations such as "Lifeguard Polish" or "Simoniz Cleaner" which are mild cutting agents. In very stubborn cases, such as deep scratches, cellulose cutting paste can be used, but with these cutting agents great discretion should be used as you will be removing some of the thickness of the paint and with continued cutting you will eventually go right through to the undercoat. After cutting always finish with wax polish and with all polishing use dry, clean and soft materials as this, in addition to the muscular effort, has a great bearing on the final finish.

As we mentioned earlier in this chapter polishing preparations should not be used on fabric covered bodywork. Such fabric may have a nitrocellulose or a p.v.c. finish, but in either case should the necessity arise, grime which cannot be removed by washing should be lightly scrubbed off with soap and water and a soft brush. The only exception is that in the case of black nitrocellulose fabric roof covering we have polished with ordinary black boot polish without running into any trouble, in fact it not only imparted a very fine finish but it also appeared to keep the fabric nice and supple.

Glass should be washed with the sponge then dried with the chamois leather and polished with a soft dry cloth. We have found that "Brasso" metal polish is very efficacious in removing such dirt as smashed flies and guano which are sometimes rather difficult to get off with water alone. Tar may be removed by rubbing with a rag moistened with a little petrol and this treatment also applies to tar on cellulose paintwork. In the case of the windscreen glass it may appear perfectly clean and yet have a coating of that modern evil traffic grime, which will only show up as an opaque smear when the screenwipers are used. The most effective cleaner for this is "Screenglo" made by Trico Limited and since the grime is also deposited on the screenwiper blades they should be removed at regular intervals and washed in hot water with a little detergent added. Regular replacement of the windscreen wiper blades is a worthwhile investment, particularly nowadays as the blade becomes impregnated with diesel oil after a few months. You will have to convert a modern blade as the original patterns are no longer available but this can generally be done without too much difficulty. It is very easy to cut down the length of a blade if the modern replacement is too long by laying it on a block of metal and cutting straight through it with a cold chisel.

The bright metal work in the early Vintage period was nickel plated with the radiators of nickel silver and in the late Vintage and P.V.T. period it was chromium plated. Certain cars had a few parts in polished stainless steel. No cars in these periods had any polished brass or copper exterior metal work except exhaust pipes.

Nickel plate will have to be cleaned with metal polish and this should be done regularly as if it is allowed to become very tarnished at the best it will be hard work to polish and at the worst you may find that it is beyond the aid of Brasso.

If you need to replate any of the metal work make sure that you use the correct plating for the period of your car.

Chromium plating and stainless steel should require only the wet chamois leather to keep them clean, you can then cover these parts over with wax when you are polishing the paintwork. If chromium plating is left uncleaned for long periods it may become covered with a brown deposit which can be removed with metal polish, or in very bad cases with steel wool and "Brasso", but this is very drastic and usually when the metal work is in this state it is time for replating. If you have a copper exhaust pipe which is badly tarnished brush on a coat of "Jenolite R.R.N.", leave this to work for some time, and then wash it off. Next give the pipe a good scrubbing with steel wool and "Brasso", clean this off and finally polish with metal polish and a soft dry duster.

Maintenance and Repair of the Main Body Frame and Dickey Seat

Motor-car bodies in the Vintage and P.V.T. period in almost every case were based on an ash framework. Since the youngest of these is now over twenty years old it is not surprising if certain faults develop and these vary from minor but very irritating squeaks to dry rot in one of the main members. Repairs to the framework are not by any means impossible but they will involve you in some rather nice carpentry and it will, of course, be necessary to remove the upholstery or body trim adjacent to the area requiring repair. The upholstery or trim may be screwed in position but it is far more likely that it is fixed in with tacks and these will possibly be rusty. Great care should be taken when removing these tacks so that the material is not damaged and you will then be able to replace the trim without any sign of the disturbance.

If the trouble is only squeaking due to loose joints the cure should be quite simple. If possible cement the joint with "Casco" glue and then if the screws are rusty use new screws. Should the holes be worn so that the screws cannot be pulled up tight you could possibly drill out the holes and fit "Rawlplugs" but take care when drilling that you do not go through the outer fabric or metal panelling of the body. When replacing any screws always use steel ones as they must be pulled up very tightly and brass screws are not strong enough. If the trouble is dry rot the entire rotten area must be cut out right back to the sound wood. If possible it is much better to remove the faulty woodwork right back to the nearest joint, as shown in fig. 11, so that when you have made the new woodwork, copying that which you have removed, it can be jointed up as before. When the repair has been completed give the new woodwork a coat of white-lead paint. If this is not possible, and you are forced by circumstances to cut through the members between the joints, use a scarfed joint for uniting the new members to the old one and this joint should be cemented and screwed. Also if it is necessary this may be strengthened with a steel plate. Should the member or members be broken but otherwise good it may be possible to cement the breaks and then to strengthen the damaged area with steel plates screwed into position. One of the most difficult parts to repair is the upright member found on either side of the windscreen on a saloon body. These members have to be strong as they not only support the front of the roof but also probably the heavy front doors in addition. If you need to replace one of these members you will almost certainly have to cut away the metal panelling or fabric covering above the waist-line. This portion of the new member when in position will have to be re-panelled or re-covered with fabric to match the body, the joints can be covered with aluminium beading, screwed into position with countersunk screws and the heads filled in with stopping before painting. It is only practicable to give a very general description of this type of repair as each one varies to such a large extent and it is only possible to plan the method of repair when the damage has been explored but we have done several such jobs with complete success.

If your car has a dickey seat, that is the occasional seat in the rear of a two-seater fitted with a lid which can be closed or when open forms the back of the seat, you will find that the lid is attached to the body with a long hinge known as a piano hinge. It is also fitted with a folding

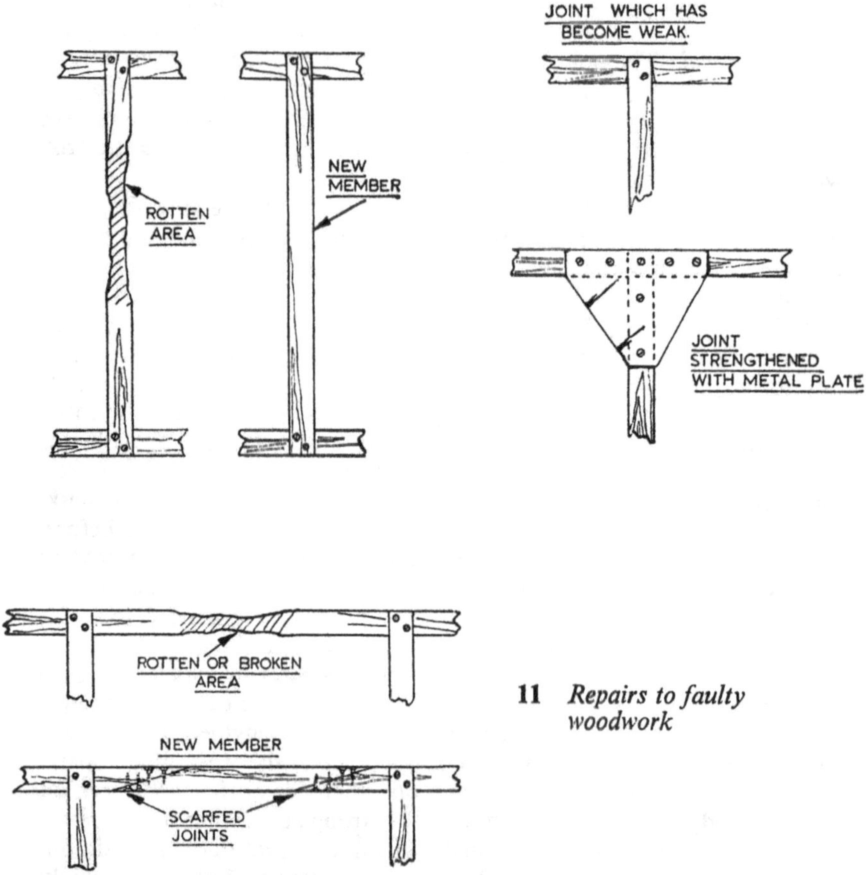

11 *Repairs to faulty woodwork*

stay on each side to retain the lid in the open position. Both fittings may be in a badly worn condition and if this is the case replacements can be obtained from Jagger Limited. It will not be any use quoting them the make of car but you must show them the old fittings and they will supply you with the nearest that they have. If the ash members to which these fittings are attached are worn, rotten or broken, they must be replaced. It is essential that this seat back is in good condition as you will realise that any passenger seated in this position is at the extreme rear of the car and should the back of the seat collapse he or she would be decanted out of the car A-over-T backwards with dire results.

Repairs to the Metal Panelling, Wings and Valances, Fabric Covering and Sunshine Roof

We have said in our previous book that large panel-work repairs which would entail a great deal of panel beating and also possibly special plant are not jobs that the average amateur can tackle with any great hope of success. However, small dents can be knocked out and then filled and any cracks welded as a first operation. Distorted mudguards can often be restored to the correct shape. A frequent fault in back mudguards is caused by the rear trailing edge having been forced inwards by such a manoeuvre as reversing into a door post, causing the valance edge to be buckled outwards at the top. This valance edge should be vertical as shown in fig 12 and never tapered outwards. To carry out this repair you will

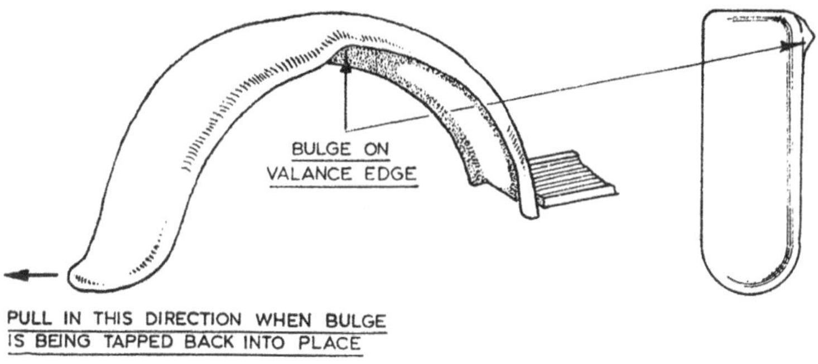

12 *Straightening a rear wing valance*

require a mate who should pull the wing backwards from the rear bottom edge while you tap the valance edge back into its correct position. You may find that the rolled-in stiffening edge of the wing has been cracked at the point of greatest distortion and if so this must be welded, otherwise the wing will always revert to its former damaged shape. After welding file down any high spots of metal, tap out any small dents and irregularities and then fill with knifing filler. When this is quite hard it should be rubbed down and if necessary re-filled and rubbed down again until the wing is the correct shape when it can be painted. Ordinary knifing filler, either oil bound or cellulose, must never be applied in one thick coat, the number of coats will depend on the depth of the dent to be filled and each thin coat must dry really hard before the application of the next one. A new filler which is much more convenient to use for small dents is Holt's "Cataloy Paste". This is in two parts which are mixed together before use and since the filler does not depend on evaporation for drying it can be put on in any thickness in one application. When the filler is hard it can be filed down to shape and then it can be rubbed down smooth with well wetted waterproof cutting paper. Very deep dents which cannot be hammered out, holes and pieces broken out of the edge castings, such as cast aluminium bonnet boards, can be filled using a Holt's "Cataloy Glass Fibre Repair Kit" or any other fibreglass repair material. Fibreglass makes a very strong repair and when it has set hard it can be filed quite readily.

If your spare wheel is carried on a bracket or at the side of the car it will probably rest in a sheet metal well sunk into the front wing or into the running board. The well should have a drain hole about ½ in. dia. as otherwise in wet weather the well will inevitably fill with water and if this is allowed to remain the metal will soon disintegrate.

We have described the re-covering of fabric bodies in our previous book and the same treatment applies to the fabric roofs of metal panelled saloon bodies. While we are on this subject we have found that when stretching the fabric over convex curves, where you will have an excess of fabric which you pull into a multiplicity of small folds, the application of the domestic electric iron is a very great help. The folds flow out as if by magic but the temperature is very critical, too low it will have no effect and if it is too high the surface will be burned off the cloth. A fair pressure on the iron is required and it should be kept in motion while it is in contact with the fabric. We should mention that we have only used this method on nitrocellulose cloth. If you have any holes or torn parts in the fabric which you would like to repair this can be done quite satisfactorily by cementing on a patch of similar material provided the body is covered with a cloth of the nitrocellulose variety such as Rexine, and this is always the case if the body has the original Vintage fabric. The procedure for patching is as follows: having cut the patch to the correct size you must next pare the edges down in a nice smooth chamfer to a feather edge working on the back of the fabric. This is done so that the patch when cemented will lie flat and not present a step due to the thickness of the cloth which would cause the patch to be ripped off when cleaning the car. The paring must be done on a hard smooth surface, such as a piece of plate glass, and a paring knife can easily be made from an old broken machine hacksaw blade about 1 in. wide, ground to a razor edge as shown in fig. 13. The cement to be used is Rawlplug "Durofix", coat the back of the patch and the area of the body fabric to which the patch is to be fixed with a nice even coat of the "Durofix". The cement is much better applied with the end of your finger as it should be rubbed out to a smooth coating. Allow the first coat to dry and then re-coat both the surfaces and apply the patch to the body while the cement is still tacky and press the patch down, particularly the edges, until the cement is dry, which will only take a few minutes. Leave the patch to dry for a few hours and then spray the area with a coat of cellulose paint. You should now have a very neat and durable repair.

Very small holes such as those left by screws which have held some fixture which you have removed, or by a cigarette burn from which incidentally we once suffered on a re-fabricked body, can sometimes be hidden by fitting a dummy domed-head stud either painted to match the fabric, polished chrome plated or made of stainless steel.

If your car is fitted with a sunshine roof which is in need of repair it will have to be removed. It is not possible to give instructions for the removal of the sliding panel as there are a number of different types of construction and locking devices, but whatever type it is it can be removed so that you will have to study its construction in the open and closed

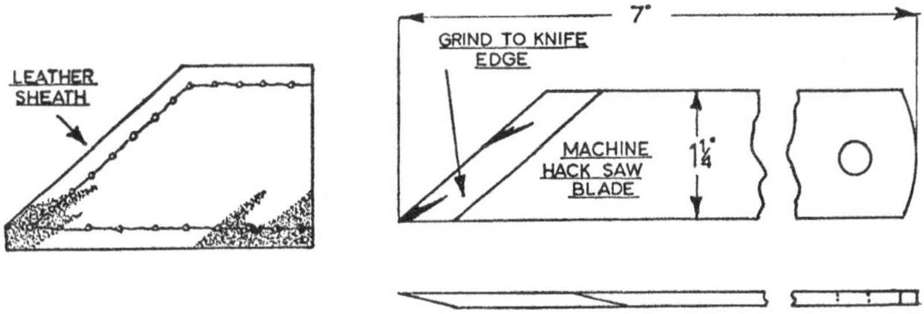

13 *Paring knife and sheath*

positions to find out how it is fixed. It may be either metal panelled or fabric covered so that repairs will be the same as we have given for the remainder of the body. If the lining is soiled but otherwise sound it may be possible to clean it with petrol or carbon tetrachloride, if not the lining is tacked in position and while the sunshine roof is off the car it is quite easy to fix new cloth to match the remainder of the head lining. The replacement of this other part of the interior trim is described in our earlier book. Clean out the channels and lubricate the slides and locking mechanism. You will find that the channels are fitted with drain tubes which pass down between the body covering and the lining. The tubes are often blocked up with dirt and it is essential that they are kept clean as otherwise rain-water may flood over into the body. The tubes were usually made in steel and so you may find them in a badly rusted state, in which case, remove them and make new ones to match from copper tube with brass flanges brazed in position. If you have a roof ventilator which is in bad condition and beyond repair replacements can be obtained from Jagger Limited.

Mudguards and their Brackets

Nothing mars the appearance of a motor-car more than mudguards that are out of line or, even worse, that are flapping about. It may be that the mudguards are in good condition but that the brackets have been bent out of the correct position. In such a case you will have to remove the mudguard concerned from its bracket and if the re-setting that is required is only slight the bracket may be bent cold in position. If however, the amount of re-forming is very extensive it will be better to remove the bracket and heat the metal before bending it making sure that the mudguards on opposite sides of the car are an equal height from the ground and the same distance from the chassis. Examine the fixing of the mudguards to the bracket and the bracket to the chassis, it is fatal if there is any lack of rigidity here as not only will there be an appalling cacophony but the paint will be cracked round the loose bolt heads. Replace the bolts which should be a good fit in their holes and make sure that the nuts are tight. With some cars the original brackets did not give enough support to the wings. If you have this trouble see if it is possible to strengthen the brackets or perhaps to fit an extra stay, but be sure if you do this that the appearance of the car is not spoiled. Rear mudguards are frequently fixed into the wheel arches with wood screws and these are often rusted away or loose in their holes. You could probably overcome this trouble by fitting larger screws or by drilling new holes in the wing between the original ones and fitting new screws. The fixing may be by coach bolts which have become loose but are rusted up solid so that the bolt rotates in its square socket. The removal of a bolt in this state often presents you with a very slow and laborious job and we have mentioned several methods of removal in our earlier book. When the old bolt is at last removed, replace it with one of the hexagon headed variety but make sure that the bolt head or nut, depending on the way you have to fit it, does not foul the tire, remembering that the wheel will come much closer to the wing when the car is in motion due to spring flexure. If you use stainless steel bolts and nuts for this repair they will never rust again.

Running Boards

Running boards were either made in wood or metal. In the Vintage period the boards were wood, but P.V.T. cars may have them made in metal. If you have a wooden running board which is in bad condition the replacement is quite a straightforward job; you should use seasoned ash. These boards were usually bolted to the brackets by countersunk-head coach bolts which were sunk in flush with the top surface of the board so that they did not show through the covering. However, it is a very poor type of bolt to use, as the countersunk-head tends to split the wood. A superior job can be made using large square-head bolts and an even better one if they are of stainless steel. To fit the bolt into the wood first drill a hole which is a close fit on the shank of the bolt, then counter-bore the hole to a diameter equal to the size across the flats of the square and to a depth equal to the thickness of the bolt head. Next place the bolt in the hole and tap it into the wood to mark the square, remove the bolt and the corners of the square can be cut out with a chisel. When you have finished the bolt head must be a tight fit in the wood. The head of the bolt should be flush with the surface of the wood, if it is below you must fill in the space with plastic wood. If the board is covered with fluted rubber you can still get this to match the original. It should be cemented to the board with black "Bostik Power Adhesive". Paint the "Bostik" onto both surfaces with a stiff brush and allow it to dry. When the two surfaces feel dry to the touch put the rubber onto the board and press it down firmly; you must place the rubber in the correct place the first time as you cannot move it once it is down. It is therefore better to have the rubber a little oversize and to trim it to size after the "Bostik" has set. When the rubber sheet has been fitted, place the two running boards face to face, clamp them together and then leave them for a few hours for the "Bostik" to set thoroughly. The right-angle ribbed aluminium beading can also be obtained easily and this should be cut to size and mitred neatly at the corners, fix the beading with countersunk raised-head screws either in plated brass or stainless steel. The rubber covering can be polished up with a stiff brush and black shoe polish in a most gratifying manner. Aluminium ribbed sheet can also be obtained in different patterns so that if you have to replace such a covering you should be able to match it. This sheeting is tacked into place under the angle beading. Aluminium can be cleaned with soap and water and a brush or, if it is in a very bad state, with a wire brush. Polish it with "Brasso".

Vintage cars frequently had the tool box and the battery box fitted on, or in, the running board. It was also popular in this period to have a fitting on the running board to hold a standard two-gallon petrol can. If your car has such a fitting do not leave it empty but find a can painted in the correct petrol company colours and mount it in the bracket. Repairs to the battery or tool box are straightforward carpentry and the boxes should be painted to match the body or mudguards.

Some types of metal running boards were covered in fluted rubber cemented in position. Straight boards are quite easy to re-cover using "Bostik", in the same way as we have described for wooden boards, but shaped running boards, which are in effect a continuation of the front mudguards, are rather more trouble as the rubber coverings were moulded. In such a case it would probably pay you to remove the old rubber, clean up the metal and paint it to match the wings, and then to fit channels and rubber strips. This is actually the final type of running board design and consisted of a sheet metal board fitted with parallel strips of aluminium channel, fixed to the running board with countersunk screws, into which rubber beading was fitted. The aluminium running board channel and the rubber filler can be obtained in two sizes, ¾ in. wide and ⅞ in. wide from Jagger Limited. The channel is now also made in stainless steel and you can get this from T. P. College. If you are re-painting this type of running board it is essential to remove the strips of channel before painting as there is a great likelihood of rust having started to form underneath.

Repairs to the Paintwork

Damaged paintwork should be repaired as soon as possible because in the case of steel panelling the naked metal will start to rust as soon as it is exposed to the atmosphere and even aluminium will corrode in time. Remove any loose paint and then rub down the surrounding paint to a feather edge and brush or spray on the primer depending on the finish; that is coach paint or cellulose, add the coats of filler and finally the colour coats. If the metal is steel and rusting has taken place, treat the area with a rust remover such as "Jenolite"; if it is aluminium use the special etching primer. If your car is finished in coach paint you cannot do any touching up with cellulose as it will react with the paint. It may dissolve it in the way a paint remover works or it will probably dry in a crows-foot pattern. Touching up should therefore be carried out in a similar type of paint to the original finish. If cracks in the paint show round beadings it is no use touching them up until you have eradicated the cause, which is sure to be due to looseness of the beading. You will have to find the screws that hold the beading in place which will be hidden by stopping, but if they are loose they will probably show through the paint. Re-fit the beading securely before you carry on with the painting.

The underside of mudguards and running boards should be kept clean and treated with a very tough type of paint to resist the chipping and abrasion of flying stones and mud.

We have described the different types of paint and the methods of application in our first book. If you have to repaint the car, and of course this will be necessary some time however meticulous you have been with the cleaning and polishing, do use a colour which was typical of the period and not a modern colour scheme. For instance, in the Vintage era many cars had black stove enamelled mudguards and valances and very rarely were they painted in more than one colour other than a combination of one colour and black.

The Hood Frame and Fabric

The hood frame consists of ash sticks connected together and anchored on to the body by a fairly elaborate mechanism made from strip steel. The steel strips are riveted together and the wood, when erected, is usually clamped to the top of the windscreen by thumb screws. Examine the wood screws attaching the ash sticks to the steel mechanism which must be tight. The rivets in the mechanism are another source of trouble and when these have been worn loose the result is an unholy rattle, the only cure for which is to take off the mechanism, cut out the old rivets and reamer out the holes to fit oversize rivets. Make sure that the frame is a good fit on the brackets that project from each side of the body at the rear, and have a good look at the clamping brackets that hold the frame to the top of the windscreen; these are usually held on by two wood screws which eventually become loose. If this is the case and they will not remain tight, try to arrange a firmer type of fixing as it is very disconcerting and expensive to have the wood rip away in a high wind. If you are sufficiently unfortunate to have a broken hood stick do not try to repair it as this will probably be unsatisfactory and may be more trouble than making a new one. Do not attempt the bending of the wood yourself, as although this has undoubtedly been done in the amateur workshop, it is very tricky and a certain amount of plant is necessary. Normally when bending anything the centre line is the neutral axis, the material on the outside of the bend will be stretched and on the inside of the bend it will be compressed. However, wood can only be stretched a very small amount and after this point has been reached fracturing takes place. It can be compressed without any disadvantage, and therefore, when bending wood a jig has to be used to cause the entire area of the wood in the bend to be in compression. You can obtain ash members in the rough, bent to your dimensions which you can get from the old stick, from Rudders & Paynes Limited or Hopton & Sons. Send them a drawing and have the section a little larger than the old stick. Spoke-shave the stick to shape and sandpaper it to a very smooth surface. You can finish it either in yacht varnish or good quality enamel. You may of course, have to untack the material from the broken stick, this will depend on which stick is damaged but take care when removing the tacks and the cloth should then be able to be refitted without any trouble. Hood sticks can also be made by the lamination process described in our other book. The steel mechanism is often very rusty and in such a case it should be removed from the sticks, well cleaned with a wire brush and then given two coats of enamel. If you take this mechanism to pieces make a drawing before you knock out the rivets or otherwise you may get in a great tangle when the time comes to re-assemble it. Also while it is dismantled you might like to have it dull chromium plated and then fit it together with stainless steel rivets.

The hood fabric can be cleaned with new bread. Take half a loaf and rub the cloth with the cut end and as the bread gets dirty cut off a slice and then proceed until the whole area of the hood has been cleaned. If the fabric is still good but has any holes in it due to chafing on the hood sticks these can be patched with similar material. The patch should be cemented in position with Dunlop upholstery solution L.107, both surfaces of the joint should be coated and then allowed to dry before pressing them together. The patch must then be handstitched with linen thread.

If the hood fabric is perished it should be replaced; you must use double-texture hood cloth. Do not use a modern p.v.c. cloth as it will be an anachronism on a pre-war car. It is quite possible for the amateur to save a great deal of cash by carrying out his own re-covering of the hood but the difficulty lies in the stitching and unless a fairly heavy machine is available it is almost impossible. If, however, you do try to do it yourself the stitches should be about six to the inch and you will require No. 30 linen thread and a size 22 needle but neither of these can be used on the average domestic machine.

CHAPTER VII

MAINTENANCE OF THE ELECTRICAL EQUIPMENT

If the engine is the heart of a motor-car then the electrical equipment is the nerve centre. When properly maintained the majority of electrical accessories are very reliable, but their routine inspection and upkeep are essential not only to the efficient running of the car but to the elimination of faults which can be more irritating than almost any other defects which are likely to occur in the vehicle. We frequently see the most pleasant motor-cars with the tattiest wiring imaginable and this state of affairs inevitably leads to trouble. It may only result in difficulty with engine starting or in dim lights but it can also lead to a complete breakdown at the most inconvenient time which could otherwise have been avoided by a little thought and energy expended at a more opportune moment.

The Magneto

By the beginning of the Vintage era magnetos had become very reliable pieces of electrical equipment and for that reason many cars are still working happily with their original instrument. Consequently the magneto is often taken for granted and left unattended for years. A routine check-up about once a year should give adequate warning if trouble is pending and allow the necessary repairs to be effected in the comfort of the motor house instead of in a dark and wet lay-by on a cold winter's night.

It is generally more convenient to work on a magneto when it has been removed from the engine and most magnetos are fairly easy to dismount. Always mark the timing before removing the magneto, both at its drive connection and at the distributor, to avoid replacing it one complete revolution out of time. Hold the magneto gently in the vice and rotate its shaft slowly by hand when you should feel a very definite resistance to rotation twice per revolution. If you do not then the instrument probably needs remagnetising but go through the rest of the maintenance before coming to a definite decision. When gripping the magneto in the vice do not let the steel vice jaws touch the magnets as this will short circuit the magnetic field and no electrical generation will take place. It is best to use fibre or lead jaws in the vice for this purpose.

Next examine the contact breaker points which is best done by taking the complete contact breaker assembly out of the magneto and then removing the moving contact arm. Magnetos have platinum contacts which are much softer than the tungsten points found on coil ignition breakers and they can be filed to remove any pitting or piling which has occurred. Take very great care to file away only the minimum amount of platinum from each point to render it clean and flat. Use a super-fine file and never use emery cloth, as it is very difficult to produce a flat surface with such material. Examine the return spring which should not have any severe bends in it, as such kinks will generally lead to a breakage. Also look at the fit of the rocker arm on its fulcrum pin. Up to 0·003 in. of wear is permissible at this point but more than that will give a varying gap and varying timing over the range of engine speed. Some types of points, springs and rockers are still available through automobile electrical stockists such as Electrical Services (B'ham) Limited, as are many other Vintage magneto spares. If the rocker bush is worn but its pin is in good order a new bush can easily be made from Tufnol which is better than the orginal fibre as it does not swell in damp weather.

Now check the fit of the cam ring on its spigot. It should be free to turn over the range of advance and retard but it should have no play. Wear at this point can sometimes be taken up by setting up the end cover of the magneto in a lathe, skimming the spigot then soldering on a ring of brass about $\frac{1}{16}$ in. thick and remachining the spigot to a nice fit in the cam ring. Examine the carbon brush in the back of the contact breaker plate which should be clean and properly spring loaded against the face of the magneto end-plate. This brush is part of the low tension circuit of the magneto and resistance in its contact will give a marked falling-off in performance.

The contact breaker can now be assembled back into the magneto with a smear of oil on the moving parts. The contacts should be set to a gap of 0·012 in. when fully open and this should be checked on both cams. If there is a difference of gap which cannot be rectified, set the contacts to a minimum opening of 0·012 in.

Next clean the inside of the distributor and examine the inner surfaces for traces of electrical tracking. In some cases these may be removed by judicious cutting with fine emery cloth and metal polish but the surface must be left highly polished or the trouble will quickly recur. Polish the brass segments with metal polish and clean up the rotating contact if it is metal. In the case of a carbon distributor brush examine this for remaining length of life and if necessary replace it. Lastly put a drop of oil on the distributor spindle, a lubrication point is usually provided for this purpose, and reassemble the magneto. If now there is still no stiff reaction to turning by hand, and consequently a poor spark at low speed, take the magneto to a service station for remagnetising which should only be done with the magneto fully assembled.

It should only be necessary to strip the magneto any further than just described to repack the armature bearings with H.M.P. grease every 5 years or 50,000 miles. If the armature is removed for any reason always put an iron keeper across the magnet poles before drawing-out the armature as otherwise you must remagnetise the magneto after re-assembly. Also be sure to remove the high tension pick-up brush generally situated at the drive end of the magneto. Failure to do this will result in the slip ring being broken when the armature is removed. Holding the magneto in the vice and gripping the two ends of the magnet will act as a keeper while the armature is being withdrawn but a piece of iron must then be put across the inside of the armature tunnel before removing the magneto from the vice. Should the armature bearings be worn or corroded replacements are available from the Hoffmann Manufacturing Co. Limited who have agents in most large towns.

If you find that the contact points are pitting quickly after being cleaned then the most likely cause is a defective condenser which, in the case of a conventional Vintage magneto, is housed in the armature and will need expert attention to replace it. Another cause of point corrosion is an excess of petrol vapour finding its way into the contact breaker housing. This is generally due to the carburetter dripping onto the magneto and such a state of affairs is very dangerous in any case as it could cause a serious fire. A small drip-tray with a drain pipe leading to a safe place should always be fitted underneath the carburetter if it is located directly above the magneto.

Before refitting the magneto have a good look at the high tension leads. If there are any signs of deterioration in the insulation fit new cables, the modern p.v.c. insulated leads are a great improvement over rubber as they are oil resisting and can be kept clean. Make sure that the ignition switch lead is in good condition and if the switch itself happens to be incorporated in a switch box, or is part of a multiple switch, see that there is no possibility of the magneto lead coming into contact with a live terminal or some other part of the electrical system as this will probably demagnetise the magneto instantly and may actually burn out the armature winding.

Whenever you dismantle a magneto remember to clean the bench and the tools which you will use and to get rid of all traces of iron filings otherwise they are bound to be attracted into the magneto and are impossible to get rid of unless by demagnetising the whole instrument.

We have based our description on the conventional rotating armature magneto but if you happen to have the much rarer polar-inductor type of instrument the same principles apply although the construction is different.

The Dynamo and Starter

Both of these electrical machines share a great similarity in the maintenance necessary to keep them in good order. Firstly lubrication: wherever there is an oil can hole this must be attended to with engine oil at about 2,000-mile intervals but this lubrication must be done sparingly as otherwise the inside of the instrument will become soaked with oil—two or three drops are all that is necessary. Where there is no oiler but obviously a bearing then in all probability it will be a ball race packed with grease which can only be attended to by stripping the machine. Such bearings only need attention at very widely spaced intervals of say once every five years, then pack them with H.M.P. grease.

The brushes and the commutator of both starter and dynamo need attention about every 10,000 miles. The whole inside of the commutator end of the machine gradually accumulates a deposit of powdered copper and carbon which are both conductors of electricity. It is therefore essential to clean away this deposit to avoid surface leaks which contribute to a lowering of the efficiency. Examine the brushes for their fit in the brush holders which should be a free sliding one. See that the brushes have not worn down to the point where their springs can no longer bear properly and so keep the brush in proper contact with the commutator. New brushes are now extremely difficult to obtain in the sizes to suit pre-war cars but it is a fairly simple matter to get the next modern size larger and to file it down until it fits your brush-holder. Make sure that the flexible brush leads cannot touch the dust cover or the frame when the brushes are in place.

The commutator can generally be cleaned quite satisfactorily by using a cloth soaked in petrol on a wooden stick inserted between the brush-holders and then rotating the armature by hand, repeating the operation with clean portions of rag until the commutator is clean. If petrol will not remove all the dirt metal polish can be applied in a similar way, finishing with a dry cloth. Do this with the brushes out and on no account use emery cloth as the emery will become embedded in the copper and will wear away the brushes very quickly.

The brush springs normally last for ever but trouble can be experienced due to a spring, which has been excessively deformed by a clumsy electrician, not exerting the correct pressure on its brush. The correct loading depends upon the area of contact of the particular brush but it is based upon a minimum pressure of 3½ lb. p.s.i. between the brush and the commutator. If the commutator is badly scored then it must be set up in a lathe and skimmed, the insulating separators being cut back below the level of the commutator bars. See that all dust covers are properly in place and are a good fit as dirt getting into the brush gear will cause excessive wear and poor performance.

Next check all the wiring connections. Remember that the starter motor takes a very heavy current and that a small electrical resistance is enough to cut down its performance considerably. In the case of rubber mounted engines it is equally important that the engine is correctly earthed to the chassis frame, a point often overlooked. While on the subject of the heavy current taken by the starter we feel that the layout often found on early cars which has the main starter switch on the instrument panel with its consequent long leads is sometimes the cause of poor starting in cold weather. If a solenoid switch can be mounted out of sight near the motor and the main leads greatly reduced in length, the old switch can still be used to operate the solenoid resulting in better starting and no change in the appearance of the car.

The most common method of engagement between the starter and the flywheel is the Bendix drive. If you have this type of drive the screw thread should not be oiled but should be washed occasionally with paraffin. If it is oily the pinion will tend to run round with the screw instead of sliding into mesh. Most patterns of Bendix pinion are still available, should yours be worn out. It is a good idea to check the tightness of the spring-securing bolts occasionally as if these come loose the end of the armature shaft will eventually be ruined. Take a look at the teeth on the flywheel ring and see that they are still serviceable all the way round the periphery. If they are getting into a bad state do not neglect rectifying this because it is a fault which can easily break the starter motor, an expensive matter to repair.

If the starter switch can be taken to pieces this should be done very occasionally and the contacts cleaned up and this is another step towards getting the full battery voltage to the starter motor. It is important to check the state of the insulation on all main starter leads and particularly on those behind the instrument panel if your car is so fitted. A short circuit to earth here is very difficult to cope with in an emergency and some very spectacular pyrotechnic displays can take place just above your knees with dire results in a very short time.

Reverting now to the dynamo, check that the field fuse is in good condition and that its contacts are clean. This fuse normally has a 4 amp. rating should you be in any doubt, and it may be located in the fuse box, in the cut-out box, or on the dynamo itself. The great majority of Vintage cars and many P.V.T. cars are fitted with constant current output dynamos which have a third brush adjustment. The brush is located nearer to one of the main output brushes than to any of the others and moving it still nearer to that brush will increase the dynamo output. The whole concept is very unsatisfactory to anyone who has once used a car fitted with a constant voltage output dynamo, as in all modern cars, but do not feel bound to get the absolute maximum charge rate out of your dynamo. The electrical needs of many Vintage cars are very small, particularly in summertime, and overcharging will only mean that you will have to top-up the battery more often than is really necessary and will also shorten the battery's life; it may also cause overheating of the dynamo.

Remember not to run the engine with the battery leads disconnected, unless you first remove the field fuse, as this can do the dynamo considerable harm and will also damage any other electrical equipment which happens to be switched on at the time, due to an excessive rise in voltage.

Finally, make sure that the drive to the dynamo is in good order, the belt or chain correctly tensioned or the fabric couplings not breaking up, and if possible check the bearings for play before passing on to the rest of the electrical system.

The Cut-out or Voltage Control

Both these items are extremely reliable and long wearing and the less that they are tampered with the better. The cut-out should generally cut in at about 1,000 engine r.p.m. If it tends to stick in contact when the engine comes down to a tick-over then the spring has lost its tension. It may be adjustable in which case increase the tension very slightly and make a test. Too much spring tension will result in the cut-in speed being too high and a happy mean must be reached. The contacts should be cleaned very occasionally with a magneto file or extremely fine emery cloth held between the points and worked backwards and forwards with finger pressure holding the points together and with one of the battery leads disconnected.

The same remarks apply to a voltage control except that in this case not only can the cut-in speed be adjusted but also the output voltage of the dynamo by a separate adjustment. Again, the contacts should be cleaned at very long intervals and adjustments done very gradually on a trial and error basis.

The Ignition Coil and Distributor

About all that can be done to maintain an ignition coil in good order is to keep the insulated top cap clean and so see that both the low and high tension connections are tight and free from corrosion. When a coil gets to the point where its performance is in doubt there is nothing else left to do but to fit a new one, as repairs are impossible. Remember that all coils have ballast resistances fitted either internally or externally, the purpose of which is to protect the primary winding against overload if the coil is left switched on for any length of time without the engine running. The ballast resistance heats up under these circumstances and will then not pass enough current to induce a spark and the coil has to be left for some minutes to cool down before the engine can be started.

The same maintenance should be given to the distributor as we have described for the magneto except that the contact breaker gap should be set at 0·025 in. The contacts being tungsten cannot be filed but must be honed on a fine emery stone, care being taken to keep the contact surfaces flat. As the condenser is the most likely source of trouble in a coil ignition system, and is an easily detachable fitting, it is a good idea to fit a new one every few years. All distributor condensers are of approximately the same electrical capacity and you can choose the modern equivalent which best fits into your distributor. Keep the inside of the distributor cover clean and dry and examine it for cracks. These cannot be repaired and the cap must be replaced if damaged. Finally, see that the high tension leads both from the coil and to the plugs are in good fettle.

When you are servicing the distributor try pushing the cam spindle sideways to test for play in the bearing. If this is appreciable you will have a variable gap at the points and the timing will alter from cylinder to cylinder resulting in rough running and lack of power. The bearing is often unbushed and difficult to restore so that it will pay you to try to find a less worn replica of your existing distributor or to fit a modern new one. The latter course will at least ensure that spares are available for this very vital part of the ignition system and certain current models of Delco distributors are still quite indistinguishable from their Vintage counterparts. A drop of engine oil on the cam spindle and on the cam face are all the lubrication that is required.

The Fuse Box

We can never understand why so many owners of pre-war cars fitted with cartridge fuses are content to replace burnt-out fuses with pieces of twisted copper wire, generally of much too heavy a gauge, when it is so easy to repair the old cartridges. All gauges of fuse wire are available at most electrical suppliers and provided you have the old cartridge all that has to be done is to unsolder the pieces of wire out of the end caps, pass a new length of wire through and solder it in place. If the old fuses are lost then you can take the end caps off modern fuses, cut new lengths of glass tube to fit and then solder in new wire. Glass tube is available from most chemists' shops and to cut off a length you must first nick it all round with a fine triangular file. If a bending action is then applied to the tube it will readily break off cleanly at the mark and the ends can be rounded off by heating them to a red heat in a gas flame. You can actually make the end caps yourself if you have a lathe. All the above assumes that replacements for your existing fuse sizes are not still available and it is surprising what stocks of such items still do exist in the stores of garages who do not have an annual clear-out of redundant stock.

See that all the contact springs are clean and are gripping the fuses correctly and that one or two spare cartridges are carried somewhere in the car. If you are in despair about the condition of the fuse box, C.A.V. Limited still make a most elegant and Vintage-looking box with replaceable wire fuses which would make an excellent substitute.

The Lighting Equipment

As with all the electrically operated parts of your car, the most important rule of maintenance is to see that the current has the least possible resistance to overcome before getting to the point where it will be usefully employed. Any poor wiring connections or doubtful junctions with the chassis frame will result in an insufficient voltage across the actual lamp with a consequent dimming of your already limited candlepower. Remember that the brightness of the lamps varies with the square of the voltage.

Occasionally remove the headlamp fronts and examine the connections to the lamp holders. An easy test for the soundness of the earth return is to put a piece of wire across from the headlamp rim, if this is polished, to the radiator shell. Hold the wire in position with the lights switched on and if they dim when the wire is removed then their earth connection is poor. A permanent improvement can be made in such a case by soldering a wire to the outside of the lamp holder and running it down to an earthing connection on the chassis frame. The normal silver-plated reflectors found on pre-war cars usually lose a large part of their reflective power in about five years, particularly if you live in a town, but re-silvering is not an expensive proposition. Reflectors must be treated with great care and not polished in any way as this would remove most of the silver and in any case will scratch the surface. Firms specialising in silver plating reflectors advertise in the motoring journals. The cork sealing washers on lamp reflectors are absolutely essential to maintain the condition of the silver and should be replaced if you have any doubts about their sealing qualities. If your headlamps are of the dip and switch variety it is advisable to clean the plunger and the contacts of the switching mechanism occasionally. This will be found mounted inside the near-side lamp and is operated by the dipping action of the reflector. At the same time see that the spring return to the solenoid is up to strength and that it brings the reflector properly back into the up position.

Occasionally check the height and focus of the headlamp beams by shining the lights against a wall with the car on a level floor and see that you are complying with the law in this respect.

Side lamps and tail lamps suffer more from wiring and earthing defects than from any other cause. This is due to the wiring in both cases being in a very exposed position and you would do well to examine it from time to time and also to see whether it is possible to improve the protection on the wiring, particularly under the front mudguards. Rust forming inside lamps or between the lamps and their mountings is a common cause of failure with earth return systems and can be dangerous on rear lamps which you cannot see when driving. If you have just acquired your car and do not know the age of the lamp bulbs it is quite a sound idea to replace the whole lot as modern bulbs are very reliable and should give you some years of trouble-free illumination.

The Windscreen Wiper

There are many and various types of screen wiper to be found on Vintage motor-cars. Dealing with the electrical ones first these can be divided into two categories, one of which has to be spun to start it and the other which is self-starting. The former has a contact breaker and cam mechanism which should be cleaned and oiled occasionally and the latter has a conventional electric motor with a commutator and brush gear which should be maintained exactly as described for the dynamo. All electrical wipers have gearing which is grease packed and after many years' service might benefit from some fresh grease. Put a drop of oil on the spindle where it projects from the motor box to lubricate its bearing and oil sparingly any holes provided. Most old wipers were very slow in operation compared with modern types and can be unbearable in heavy rain. There are certain makes in current production which are both fast in operation and easily interchangeable with an old wiper, looking much the same in outward shape, and you will not spoil the appearance of your car if you decide to fit one of these.

Non-electrical wipers can be either suction operated or mechanically driven from the engine or gearbox. The former can often greatly benefit from a complete strip and clean followed by light oiling with a thin machine oil before reassembly. They are generally connected to the induction manifold by a length of rubber tubing which should be replaced from time to time as it slowly perishes with heat from the engine. Mechanical wipers are driven by a length of flexible drive like a speedometer cable and this needs occasional treatment by dismantling, cleaning and greasing. Molybdenum disulphide assembly paste is excellent for this purpose. The gear-boxes of such wipers benefit from periodic cleaning out and greasing.

The Horns

Broadly speaking, electric horns can be divided into two categories, those that have a conventional motor which energises a diaphragm through the medium of a ratchet wheel and those which work like an electric bell operating the diaphragm with a solenoid and contact breaker. Both types are very reliable and only need a very little maintenance. The motor-driven horn will need new carbon brushes at very infrequent intervals and should have a drop of oil at any oil hole about once a year. The high frequency horn needs a little attention to the cleaning of the contact breakers occasionally and requires no lubrication. If for any reason you have to dismantle any horn which is mounted outside the car take care to make good any jointing washers which you may have damaged as they are there to keep the rain out of the mechanism which will quickly deteriorate if not properly sealed.

The adjustment of the note on all types of horn is usually self evident but is best performed well out in the country. Whereas the strident discord of your twin Klaxons may be music to your ears, it certainly won't be to your neighbour's.

The Battery of Accumulators

Routine maintenance of the battery consists merely of keeping the top and connections really clean and regular topping up of the cells with distilled water—simple enough but rarely done properly. The electrolyte level should be inspected very regularly and kept just above the tops of the plates. There is something about the upper surface of a battery which seems to attract a particularly self-adhesive type of dirt but it is well worth keeping it really clean as this dirt is a conductor and will cause electrical surface leakage. The main connecting lugs will rapidly corrode if they are not kept greased. The corrosion easily washes off with water and the lugs should be disconnected from the battery posts and washed in a small bowl of hot water with a scrubbing brush. They should then be dried, reconnected to the battery and protected with H.M.P. grease.

If your battery appears to have reached the end of its life and quickly loses its charge it is sometimes possible to restore it, at least for a time, by the following method. Remove the battery from the car and empty out all the electrolyte. Then thoroughly wash out each cell with rain water or distilled water, repeating the filling and emptying of the cell several times until all loose solid matter has come out. If there are cracks in the black sealing compound on the top of the battery these can be welded up by the application of a hot iron to the crack. Now fill the cells with new battery acid of 1·260 specific gravity and give the battery a long slow charge. It is generally the accumulation of solid matter between the plates of a cell which causes an internal short circuit and dissipates the charge. Getting rid of this sludge may give the battery a new lease of life but you must remember that this solid matter has come out of the plates and you will not completely restore the battery by this method.

You may consider, like we do, that a battery master switch is a worthwhile adjunct to the electrical system. It is very convenient, if hidden, as an anti-theft device, and also is a much speedier way of turning off the current when doing electrical maintenance than the removal of a battery lead. The modern Lucas master switch incorporates an earthing terminal for the magneto which renders the car quite immobile if it has this form of ignition.

Never leave the battery discharged as this will lead to sulphation of the plates which is incurable and if your car is left unused for long periods either use the battery on another car or occasionally discharge and recharge it.

The Wiring

Of all the faults to be found on Vintage cars the electric wiring heads the list as the most common short-coming. We see more otherwise decently kept cars with the wiring deteriorated into an electrician's nightmare than with any other single fault. We know that it is quite a job to rewire the whole car without dismantling at least parts of it but when repairs are needed they should be done in a decently heavy gauge of wire, properly sheathed, properly clipped and properly connected at either end. Do not drape flimsy bell-wire across the engine nor wind it round the front dumbirons. Use a soldering iron where necessary to attach the proper terminals and remember that most Vintage cars were extremely carefully wired in the first place but the materials available were nothing like so good as can be obtained today.

External wiring to horns and lamps needs particularly careful attention and should be hidden wherever possible. Any wiring which passes under mudguards should always be enclosed in P.V.C. sheathing and is even better put into a metal tube. Remember that insulation of any sort deteriorates more rapidly with heat and so wiring should be kept as far away as possible from the engine and exhaust system.

A common place for fires to start is behind the instrument panel which is often a tangled mass of old and perished wiring which is not easy to replace on a Saturday afternoon. However, it can be done a little at a time and we hope that if yours is approaching its nadir you will make a resolution to do something about it.

CHAPTER VIII

THE DASHBOARD AND INSTRUMENTS

IT is our opinion that the dashboard has as much influence on the appearance of a motor-car as any other single part. A panel which is well finished and equipped with a good array of well-arranged instruments and controls can be a most pleasing sight. It is safe to say that all cars in the Vintage and Thoroughbred period were fitted with some type of dashboard; some of these, however, were very meagre in their fitments and if you are a rabid enthusiast for originality you will have to be content with this paucity, but should you be more open-minded and decide to add some further instruments and controls then do make sure that these fittings are of the correct period and that they match in style and finish the existing instruments. Do not be persuaded into fitting useless instruments for the sake of appearance. In our previous book we have given details of the procedure for re-finishing mottled aluminium and polished wood and these are the two finishes most generally found; both types should be cleaned if necessary by sponging with soap and water and then polished with a good wax polish. Other finishes of greater rarity are: leather-covered to match the trim, celluloid-covered wood and pressed steel with a painted finish. The leather-covered type should be treated in the same way as the upholstery; celluloid-covered boards or cellulose-finished pressings should be cleaned with a polish having a mild cutting action such as "Life Guard". Again finish with a wax polish.

Even the best of instruments need cleaning and oiling in time, and in our earlier book we have given the names of firms who can carry out this work. However, for those readers who have a natural aptitude for the cleaning and repairing of small intricate mechanisms we are giving drawings and descriptions of some of the more complicated instruments together with suggestions on cleaning and lubricating.

The Speedometer and Revolution Counter

These two instruments work on the same principles, the only difference lies in the markings on the dial, the speedometer reading in m.p.h. or k.p.h. and the revolution counter reading in r.p.m.; the speedometer also usually incorporates a mileage recording mechanism. It will be seen, therefore, that the following instructions will apply equally to either instrument.

These instruments were always driven by a flexible shaft rotating in a flexible tube, in the case of the speedometer the shaft usually being driven

I EVERYDAY VINTAGE CAR: *the 1926 D.I.S. Delage used by Richard Wheatley as normal transport from 1931 to 1937*

II EVERYDAY THOROUGHBRED CAR: *the 1932 16/80 Lagonda restored and used by Richard Wheatley in the early post-war period*

III *The magnetic speedometer*

IV *The chronometric speedometer*

from the gear-box by gearing but on some early cars the drive was by a belt from the back of the gear-box. Another method of speedometer drive was by gearing from a front wheel. The revolution counter is always driven from the engine. The flexible shaft should be lubricated every 5,000–6,000 miles and to do this it should be removed from the outer casing, cleaned and then well smeared with thin grease before replacing. The flexible drive does not function well and neither will it have a very long life if it is laid round curves of small radius—the more straight it can be kept the better. It should be remembered that a speedometer will only give a true reading when the motor-car is shod with the proper tires inflated to the correct pressure; smaller or under-inflated tires will cause a speedometer to give a reading in excess of that which it should be and oversize tires will result in a lower speedometer reading. These instruments are of three different types which are as follows:

THE CHRONOMETRIC TYPE, made by either Jaegar or Smith, as its name implies has a mechanism having a great resemblance to a watch; the internal arrangement of this instrument is shown in plate IV. This type usually shows very little wear after long periods of use. The mechanism can be cleaned after removal from its case with carbon tetrachloride using a camel hair brush and then the bearings only should be re-lubricated using the best clock oil. The teeth of the gear wheels must not be oiled except in the case of worm drives and these should be lubricated with a very small amount of thin grease. If the dial is to be removed it will be necessary first to take off the hand which is quite easy as it is a tight push fit on the spindle. Be careful when removing the hand to give a straight pull and so avoid bending the spindle. The glass and dial should be cleaned with soap and water, taking care not to damage the finish of the dial; if necessary touch up with paint the dial, hand and bezel using Johnson's "Matt Camera Black" paint for the background of black dials.

THE MAGNETIC TYPE consists of a circular permanent magnet driven by the flexible shaft, this magnet rotating either inside or outside a thin non-magnetic metal cup mounted in bearings and made usually from copper or aluminium. The cup is a close fit but is not in contact with the magnet, as shown in plate III. The rotation of the magnet creates eddy currents in the metal cup and causes it to be dragged round against the pull of a hair spring by an amount proportional to the speed of the magnet. In the case of the A.T. instrument the hand is attached to the metal cup; the Waltham instrument works on a slightly different principle in that figures are inscribed on the outside of the cup itself and are shown through a slot in the dial similar to the mileometer but larger. The cup should be quite free in its bearings, which should be cleaned and lubricated with clock oil. The magnet runs in ball races and these should be cleaned out and re-packed with grease. Slow reading in this type of instrument can be caused by loss of magnetism and to cure this it will be necessary to remove the magnet and to have it re-magnetised. When cleaning a magnetic speedometer the hand cannot be removed without a complete dismantling and this should not be necessary. If the dial screw is removed the dial can then be slipped out from under the hand, but great care should be taken as the hands are very delicate.

THE CENTRIFUGAL TYPE consists of a small spindle mounted in ball bearings which is driven by the flexible shaft, the spindle is fitted with lead weights hinged in position so that as the speed increases the weights tend to fly outwards and in doing so move a collar against the pressure of a spring. The movement of the collar is then conveyed by suitable gearing to the hand as shown in fig. 14. The sliding collar and the other small bearing should be quite clean and lubricated with thin oil and the ball races should be cleaned and packed with thin grease.

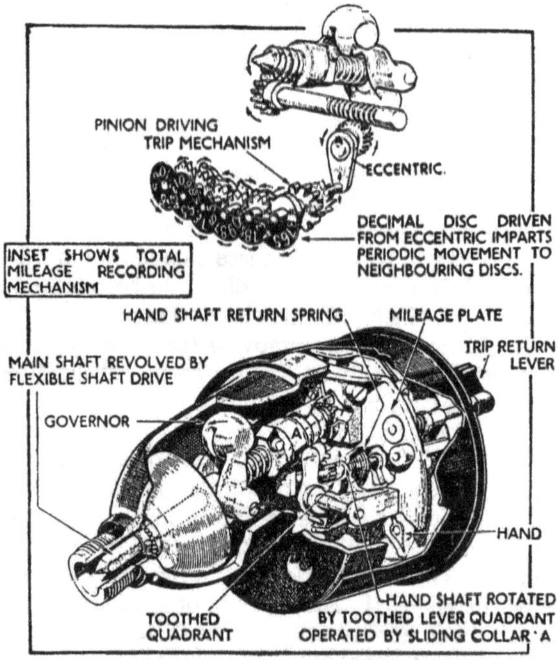

14 *Centrifugal speedometer*

Oil Pressure Gauge

All pressure gauges work on the same principle: they have a semi-circular tube of thin oval-section brass, known as a Bourdon tube, one end of which is attached to the body and the supply pipe union. The free end of tube is sealed and is attached by suitable gearing to the hand as shown in fig. 15. An increase in pressure causes the Bourdon tube to straighten and thus to rotate the spindle that carries the hand. It is unlikely that a pressure gauge will require any maintenance except perhaps cleaning and repainting. To carry out this work it may be necessary to remove the dial and therefore the hand, which is a push fit on to the tapered end of the spindle. When pulling off the hand take care not to bend the spindle. In most pressure gauges a means of adjustment will be found in the linkage to the spindle but it is not advisable to tamper with this as it was put there for setting the instrument during manufacture. If however, the hand fails to zero correctly when the engine is not running the hand should be removed from its spindle and replaced in the correct position against its stop. Some cars have a tap in the supply pipe to the gauge and this is a good thing to have as even the best of pipes can fracture and should you be unfortunate enough to suffer this breakage you can at least stop the loss of oil even if you have already spoilt her nylons. If your pressure gauge fails to function make sure, if the aforementioned tap is fitted, that it is not turned off before you start to dismantle the dashboard. After refitting an oil gauge the pipe should be bled of air by slackening the union momentarily.

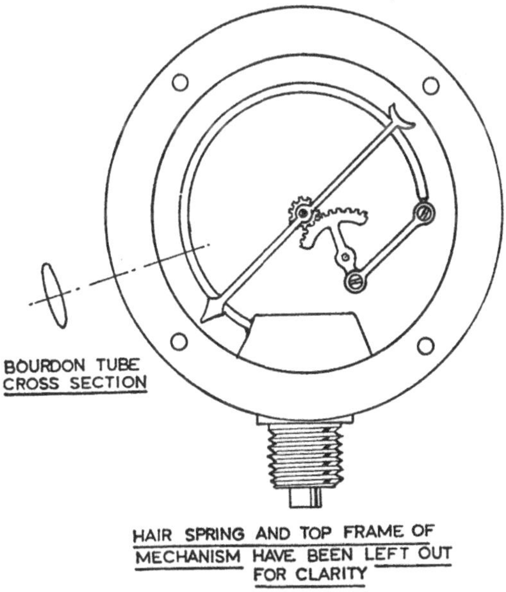

15 *Pressure gauge or thermometer mechanism*

Oil Pressure Tell-tale

Certain manufacturers, having little faith in the reliability of their oil pump but being exceedingly cheese-paring with the instrumentation, fitted a dashboard device having a small plunger which is upstanding if and when the pump functions. Such devices are generally in the form of a small spring loaded piston fitted with a leather cup washer so that an increase of pressure forces the piston forward against the spring, thus pushing the visible indicator outwards. Another arrangement has this mechanism in the crankcase and operates the plunger through a Bowden cable. The only possible cause of trouble will be a leaking cup washer which you will have to replace.

Air Pressure Gauge

If your car has its petrol fed from a pressurised tank you will have a gauge and this will be a low reading type of probably not more than 5 lb. p.s.i. The same remarks apply to this gauge as to the oil pressure gauge.

Thermometer

This instrument is in fact a pressure gauge but instead of using an external source of pressure it is self contained, the bulb, capillary tube and Bourdon tube being filled with ether and sealed. Heat applied to the bulb causes the ether to expand and the pressure in the system to rise in proportion to the temperature. The scale is usually in centigrade, boiling point is then 100°C. but it may have a Fahrenheit scale in which case the boiling point of water is 212°F. In the rather rare case of a thermometer calibrated on the Réaumur scale the boiling point is 80°R. It follows that our remarks with regard to pressure gauges apply equally to thermometers, but it should be stressed that the capillary tube cannot be shortened and if it is broken the instrument will be useless and beyond the repair of a home workshop. A thermometer in the cooling system is a very useful instrument and they were frequently fitted to the better cars in the Vintage and Thoroughbred periods. A more uncommon use is one fitted in the sump to record the temperature of the oil in which case a reading of 110°C. will indicate trouble. Such an instrument is particularly useful to avoid disaster if the car is used on a motorway or in competition, when the throttle is kept open continuously for far longer periods than it would have been in the day of the car's manufacture. It is also useful at the other end of the scale to note the normal running temperature of the oil which should be a minimum of 70°C., the free-steaming temperature of the normal diluents which find their way into the sump when the engine is cold and whose presence is adverse to the good internal maintenance of the moving parts.

Ammeter

Ammeters are of two types, moving coil and moving iron, the former is by far the better instrument but is only likely to be found on the more expensive cars. Early cars were fitted with an ammeter showing charge only but later types have a scale showing charge and discharge. No maintenance is necessary with these instruments except that with the double scale type it may be necessary to zero the needle. In the case of the moving iron type zeroing can only be done by bending the needle, if however, it is necessary to alter the setting of an ammeter of the moving coil

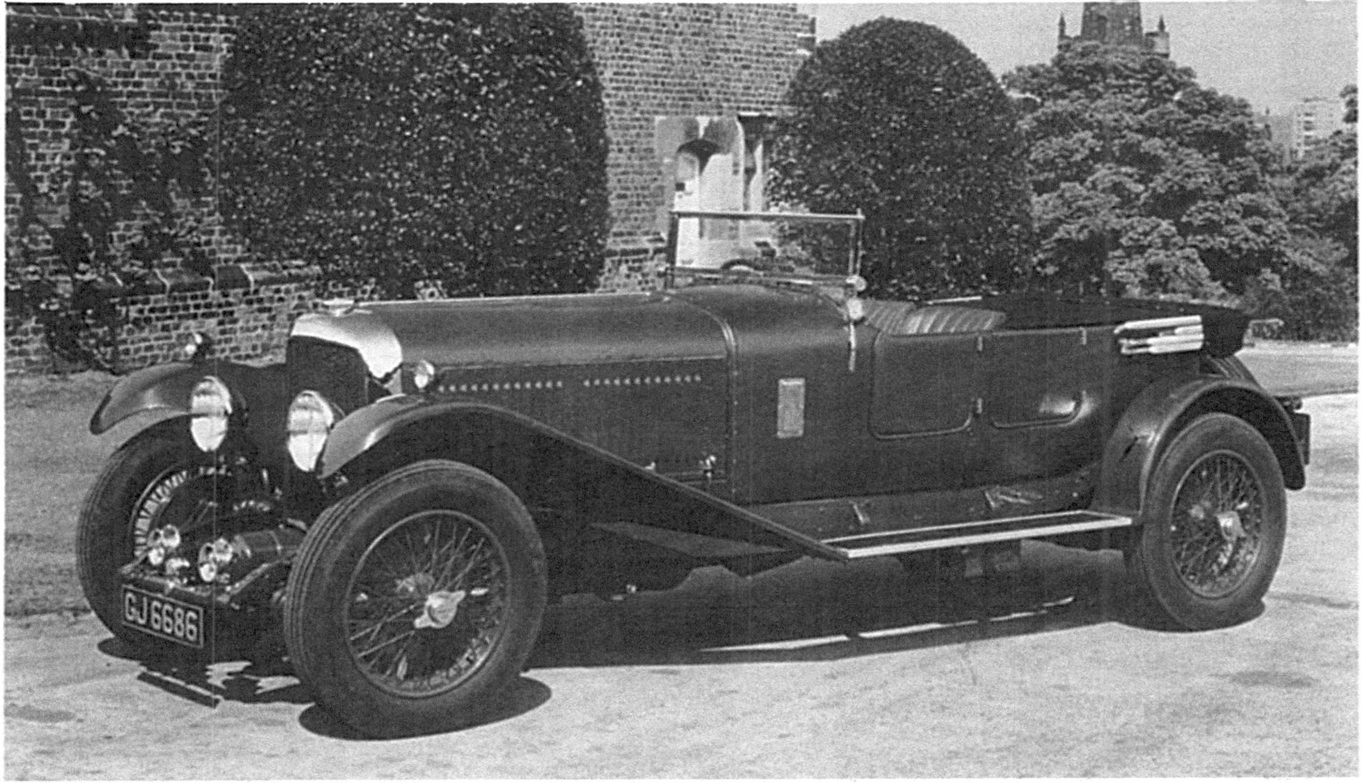

V *The 1930 Speed Six Bentley, with replica Vanden Plas coachwork, restored by Brian Morgan, 1959–1963*

VI, VII PREPARED FOR A CONCOURS: *1937 Phantom III Rolls-Royce restored to its original condition in 1961, and its interior*

type there is an adjustment provided. The means of adjustment consists of a small lever projecting downwards from the needle anchorage and the lever is sometimes operated by a small slotted screw which projects through the dial glass. This adjustment works on the same principle as the regulator on a watch, that is, by tightening or loosening the main spring, caution should therefore be used in its use. Great care should also be taken if it is necessary to remove the glass to repaint the dial as these instruments are very delicate.

Battery Capacity Indicator

This instrument is really a voltmeter but the dial, instead of being marked in volts, is divided up into different coloured sections which indicate the state of the charge. It should not require any maintenance.

Clocks

Usually clocks will have spring movements although a few cars in the later part of the period were fitted with electric movements. Both types will require some attention at fairly infrequent intervals. To clean the movement a camel hair brush and carbon-tetrachloride should be used and when all the dirt and old oil has been removed lubricate with clock oil. Both types are fitted with a regulator. A rather obvious point, but one which seems not to occur to many people, is that the local watch repairer is just as able to repair or to adjust your car clock as he is to work on household timepieces and he may be quicker than the original maker's service department.

The Sight-Glass Petrol Gauge

There were several types of petrol gauge mounted on the dashboard of which the simplest form was the Benton & Stone sight glass as fitted to the Vintage Morris. This type showed the contents of the tank by a column of petrol in a glass tube similar to the water level gauge on a boiler, the bottom of the glass tube had to be level with the bottom of the tank so that the gauge could only be used with a bulkhead mounted tank. No maintenance is necessary except that the glass may require cleaning in time. If the gauge is dismantled for cleaning make sure, on re-assembling, that a good joint is made at the bottom of the glass tube otherwise the occupants of the front seat will have a petrol bath. Cork is the only material for making this joint.

The Hobson Telegauge

This gauge has no mechanical moving parts. It consists of two components, the indicating unit mounted on the instrument board and the

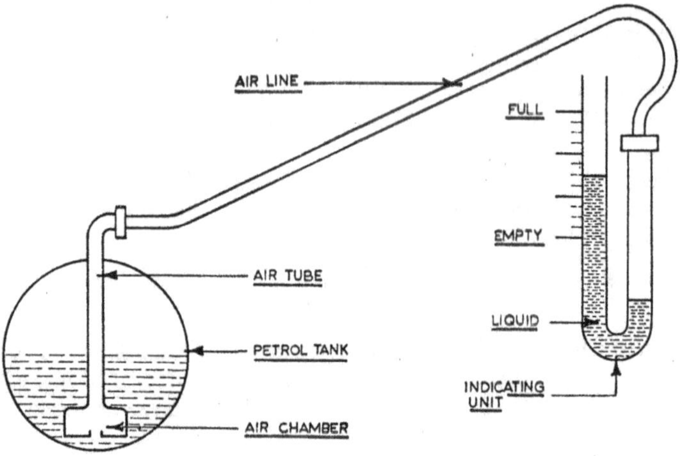

16 *Simple telegauge in operation*

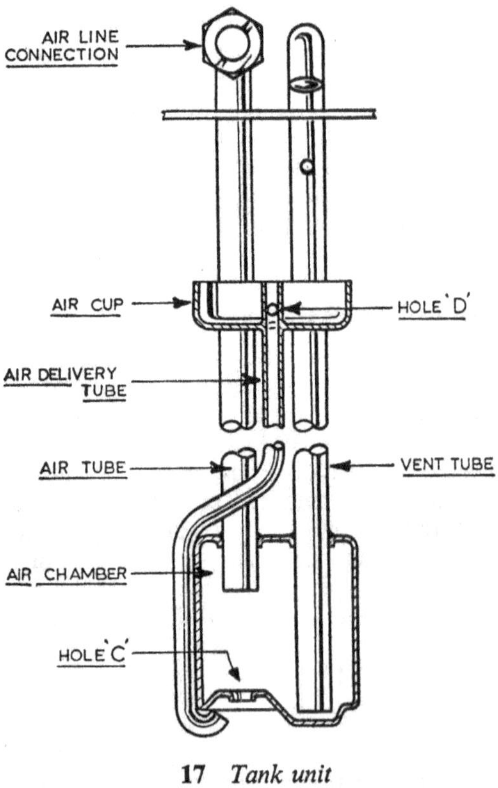

17 *Tank unit*

tank unit, connected together with a small bore pipe as shown in fig. 16. The tank unit consists of an air chamber and air tube as shown in fig. 17. The indicating unit, as shown in fig. 18, is made up in the form of a "U" tube containing a special heavy red liquid. One half of this "U" tube is of glass, open at the top end and visible on the instrument board together with the scale marked off in gallons and litres, the other half being of brass and acting as a reservoir. The calibrating wires in the reservoir are used to compensate for differences in the bore of the glass tube. During the process of filling the tank, the increasing head of petrol exerts a pressure on the air in the air tube through the air chamber which is open to the tank through the hole "C". This pressure is exerted through the air line to the indicating unit and causes a rise in the red liquid in the glass tube. Conversely, as the amount of petrol in the tank decreases the air pressure is lowered and the red liquid falls in the glass tube, thus indicating the amount of fuel in the tank. The bent tube, open at the top, is a safety device to protect the gauge against excessive pressures. The remainder of the tank unit, namely the air cup and air delivery tube, act only as a means of supplying air to the air chamber to overcome any loss of air due to absorption in the petrol or contraction caused by a drop in temperature. The air

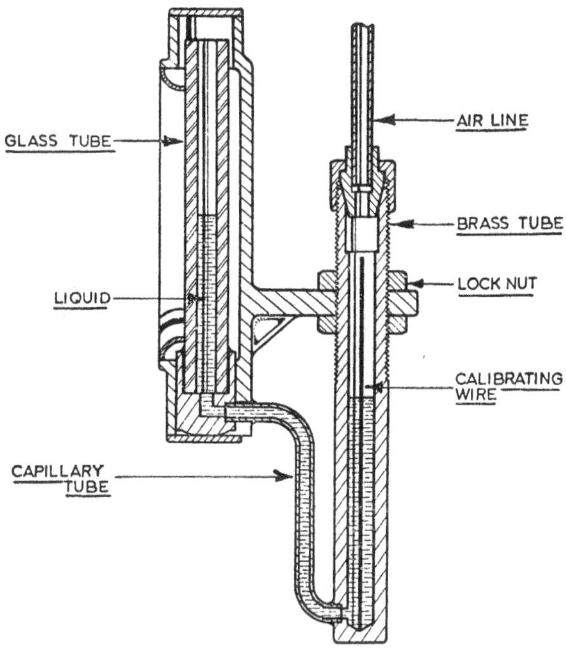

18 *Indicating unit*

supply to the tank unit is obtained by making use of the movement of the petrol in the tank. The air cups are constantly being filled by the splash of the petrol when the car is in motion. This petrol flows through the drain hole "D" and down the air delivery tube, drawing with it bubbles of air which are released at the bottom of the tube under the air chamber, entering the latter through hole "C" and displacing any petrol which may be in the air chamber. When the air chamber is full of air, any further air passing down the tube is released into the tank. When this type of fuel gauge was fitted to a Rolls-Royce it was provided, as a refinement, with a small hand pump located near the indicating unit. The hand pump, when operated, fed air into the stand pipe independently of that supplied automatically and enabled a correct reading of the gauge to be given under all conditions. No harm will result from excessive use of the pump but no useful purpose is served by operating it more than the amount required to fill the air chamber. In addition to the hand pump this model also had a pressure balance pipe between the top of the fuel tank and the top of the "U" tube. For the correct functioning of the telegauge it is essential that the red liquid in the "U" tube is set at the bottom line of the scale when the air line is disconnected, the air line must be entirely free from leaks or obstruction and the small holes in the tank unit must be free of gummed petrol. If it is necessary to replenish the red liquid it can be obtained from John Aronson Limited. The liquid should be inserted a spot at a time in the top of the brass tube after the air line has been disconnected and if, after filling, a little too much has been put in the most simple way to remove the excess is by the use of a matchstick but take care not to disturb the calibrating wires. Never slacken the locknuts or alter the position of the brass tube; if the glass tube has become stained it should be dismounted from the body of the unit and very carefully cleaned. If the calibrating wires have been lost it will be necessary to experiment with wires of different diameter until each gallon of petrol put in the tank shows an increase of one division on the sight glass. Should it be necessary to blow out the air pipe disconnect it from the indicator unit and blow from this end using a tire pump for this purpose, having first removed the petrol filler cap from the tank as a safeguard against over pressurising the tank.

The Nivex Gauge

The Nivex gauge consists of three parts: the dashboard indicator unit which is really a very sensitive pressure gauge similar to an aneroid barometer, a small spring loaded air pump also fitted on the dashboard and a stand pipe fitted into the fuel tank. Both the indicator unit and the air pump are connected to the stand pipe by separate small bore pipes. To take a reading of the contents of the fuel tank the knob of the hand pump is withdrawn to its full extent and then released. As the pump returns slowly under the action of the spring, air pressure is created in the stand pipe in proportion to the depth of the fuel in the tank and this pressure is shown on the gauge as the tank contents until the pump has completed its return stroke, when the needle returns to zero. The Nivex gauge does not require any maintenance but the joints in the piping must be completely air tight and, of course, free from any obstruction. The gauge is fitted at the back with a small knurled knob which, if necessary, can be rotated in the direction required to position the needle on the zero mark—clockwise to decrease the reading, anti-clockwise to increase the reading.

The Electric Petrol Gauge

The electric petrol gauge consists of two parts: the dashboard meter and the tank unit. The best type of meter consists of two coils placed so that they exert a magnetic force on a soft iron armature, which is mounted on a spindle with the pointer that indicates the contents of the tank on the dial. One of the coils tends to hold the pointer in the mid-position, the second coil causes the pointer to be deflected according to the amount of fuel in the tank. The instrument is usually brought into operation when the ignition is switched on and then the first coil is connected to the battery, the deflecting coil is connected to the tank unit. The tank unit consists of a potentiometer rotated by a float and gearing so that electrical pressure is applied to the deflecting coil in the meter in accordance with the amount of fuel in the tank. The advantage of using two coils is that the accuracy of the instrument is not upset by fluctuations of battery voltage. This instrument should not require any attention but if it should fail this may be due to a blown fuse, a break in the wiring or the float jammed due to gum from old petrol (see fig. 19).

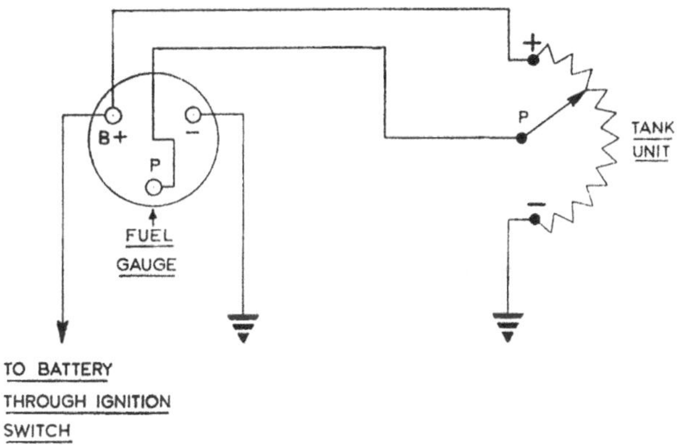

19 *Fuel gauge wiring diagram*

Air Pump

If the car is fitted with a fuel supply from a pressurised tank an engine driven pump or exhaust pressure may be used, but in either case the system will be fitted with a hand pump to give the initial pressure for starting. The plunger in the hand pump is fitted with a leather cup washer and this washer must be kept supple and lubricated but only animal fat should be used for this purpose. There is a spring loaded non-return valve in the end of the pump, the spring must be in good condition and the valve and its seat free from dirt or gumming.

Kigass

This is a small hand pump for injecting petrol into the inlet manifold for easy starting in cold weather. The pump spindle is fitted with a knurled knob at one end and at the other end a screw thread and needle valve so that the plunger must be unscrewed before it can be withdrawn. The pump is not fitted with a cup washer but has a plain plunger sealed by a gland at the flange mounted end of the cylinder. At the opposite end of the cylinder is the screwed-on base which contains two non-return valves which must be kept clean and free from gumming due to stale petrol. If the plunger is too stiff it may be lubricated with graphite when in the withdrawn position. After the pump has been used it must always be screwed down firmly.

Switches

The contacts in all types of switches should be kept clean and free from corrosion and while some lubrication is necessary this should be kept to a minimum as oil and grease are good insulating mediums. If spring contacts are broken and a replacement switch cannot be obtained, new contacts can be made using hard brass or copper. All terminals should be kept tight.

Panel Mounted Controls

Certain controls were sometimes fitted on the dashboard, such as the carburetter mixture control, the ignition advance and retard lever, the carburetter flooder knob, the radiator shutter and scuttle ventilation controls. Such controls should be kept clean and lubricated, there should be no lost motion and any worn bearings on fulcrum points should be repaired to prevent any unpleasant rattles and to make them precise in their movement.

Anti-theft Devices

Although the Vintage or Thoroughbred car is not so likely to attract the attention of a car thief as a post-war model, due to its rather conspicuous appearance and difficulty of selling without risking awkward questions, it could become the victim of a joy-rider and suffer irreparable damage. It is very difficult to protect a car against a determined professional thief but the joy-rider will most likely be put off by any type of device which will cause him inconvenience.

If your car is an early model with a closed type of body it may not be fitted with door locks. Yale make mortice locks for this purpose which can be fitted into one of the doors, while flush fitting bolts can be fitted to the other doors.

The battery master switch which cuts off all the electric power is a good device to immobilise the car if fitted in an inconspicuous place but, of course, this cannot be used if the car is parked at night on the road. However, it is an excellent fitting which we would always recommend as a safety precaution when work is being done on the car and to prevent interfering clots from operating the electrical accessories.

The Petromag is a device made by Ross Courtney which not only immobilises the ignition but also incorporates a tap which shuts off the petrol supply and so makes it very difficult to circumvent without a great deal of work and trouble. Warning—don't drop the key down the drain or you may be run-in for trying to move your own car.

The Watchdog is made by Vendik and consists of a loud horn which gives an intermittent warning. The unit should be fixed in an obscure position and it is set by a secret switch which causes the warning to sound if the ignition is switched on.

The Lander is a unit which is fitted with a key and should be installed in an inconspicuous position. When set it causes the horn to be sounded if the ignition is switched on.

A quite inexpensive system can be made up by using a Lucas Anti-Theft Master Switch—No. S.45. This switch can be fitted either inside or outside the car and is used to set the system which consists of a number of small switches fitted to the doors, the bonnet, the handbrake or even the gear-box when in the reverse position, so that when the master switch is set should any of these switched parts be moved by an unauthorised person, then the horn will be sounded. The small switches can be of the type fitted to modern car doors to operate the interior light—Lucas Model 94—both they and the wiring should be fitted in unobtrusive and inaccessible positions. If a certain amount of ingenuity is used a very good and inexpensive system can be evolved. The car horn should, if necessary, be changed for one of a continuously rated pattern.

CHAPTER IX

CARE OF THE CAR WHEN LAID UP

We realise that many Vintage and Thoroughbred cars are driven regularly throughout the year. This is an excellent thing as while they must be preserved we should not like to see them all as static Museum pieces for the remainder of their lives. However, some owners lay their cars up in the winter months, and others who have more than one desirable motor-car may need to lay up one or more of them while others are being used. If the car is not to deteriorate it is worth while taking a certain amount of care and trouble in the preparation for its period of inactivity. The instructions in this chapter should ensure that the car is not impaired by its period of hibernation, but a great deal will depend on the conditions in the motor-house or place of storage and also on the attention that the car receives during this period. Do not, therefore, prepare the car, cover it with a dust-sheet and leave it undisturbed until it is again wanted, but examine it at regular intervals to make certain that the good condition is being maintained.

Bodywork

Before laying up the car it should be thoroughly washed down and the paintwork inspected for any rust patches or potential defects. It is very much better to deal with these before storing the car than to leave them until the next time the car is wanted when they will probably have become a great deal worse. It is also pleasant to feel that the car is put away in a condition to take the road again whenever you need it. Any rust patches should receive the full treatment of anti-rust primer, filler and finish and the paintwork should then be given a good application of first-class polish.

All bright parts, excepting those which are chromium plated, should be lightly smeared with grease or vaseline. The chomium plated parts should merely be well washed and can be wax polished with the rest of the body-work.

The carpets and upholstery should be well brushed and cleaned and then the carpets treated with a good anti-moth preparation. Leather upholstery should be treated with Connolly's "Hide Food" to keep it soft and in good condition.

The car should be stored in a dry well ventilated garage which, if possible, is at least slightly heated in the winter months. If the car is an open model the hood should be erected, if it is a closed model all the windows should be left open a little way so that fresh air can circulate inside the body.

Should the garage or store place be liable to dampness there will be a risk of damage to the upholstery due to the formation of mildew. To avoid this trouble close all the windows and ventilators of a closed car and place an open box of drying agent, such as calcium chloride or silica-gel inside the bodywork to absorb any moisture, the drying agent must be renewed when it has reached saturation point. Since this procedure cannot be carried out with an open car it is a good principle to remove any carpets and loose upholstery, seats, cushions and squabs and to store these in a drier and warmer part of the premises.

The Petrol System

The petrol system should be drained and dried out from the tank to the carburetter and this work should be carried out very thoroughly to prevent the formation of a gum deposit which causes a great deal of trouble and is so difficult to remove. The carburetter, filter and petrol pump should be throughly cleaned out, the petrol tank and autovac, if one is fitted, should be completely drained and the pipes blown out with compressed air if possible. If you do not have a supply of compressed air a foot pump for tire inflation would do the job quite well.

Cooling System

It is rather better not to drain the cooling system as corrosion is liable to take place if it is left for long periods in the empty state. An anti-freeze solution should be used and the best substance for this is ethylene glycol BS.3150 in the correct strength to give complete protection from freezing. We can also recommend Smith's "Bluecol" as an alternative corrosion and frost inhibitor. Remember that a solution of ethylene glycol is more searching than plain water so that any leaks must be attended to before filling up with this mixture.

The Battery

Batteries are liable to deteriorate very quickly when they are not in use unless they are well looked after. It should also be remembered that they must be stored in a frost-proof place, otherwise they are likely to freeze up during very severe weather and should this happen it would probably result in a total loss. There are two methods of storage, in the first of which the battery may be left on the car and it can then be used for the periodical rotation of the engine and transmission. The exterior of the battery should be thoroughly cleaned and dried and topped up with distilled water, then given a full charge. After this it is only necessary to give a little use every four weeks by turning the engine over once or twice with the starter, followed up by a topping up charge. The state of the charge may be ascertained by the use of a hydrometer. Do not forget to keep the acid level topped up with distilled water.

The second method necessitates the removal of the battery from the car. First clean the exterior of the battery, check that the acid is at the correct level and give it a full charge. Next, all the acid should be emptied out and the cells washed out with distilled water which should be done three times, and each time the water should remain in the cell for about one hour. After this the cells may be filled with distilled water, the plugs replaced, the exterior thoroughly dried and the battery can then be stored in a warm dry place.

Engine and Transmission

The engine, gear-box and rear axle should be drained when hot and then refilled with fresh oil of the correct grade. The sparking plugs should be removed and a little oil injected into each cylinder. Then the crankshaft should be turned a few times to distribute the oil over the cylinder walls. The exterior of the engine should be thoroughly cleaned and then sprayed with thin oil to prevent corrosion of any of the polished parts, particularly aluminium castings. An easy way to do this is to thin down engine oil with two parts of petrol to one of oil and to spray the mixture onto the engine with a disinfectant or horticultural spray. The clutch should be propped out sufficiently to prevent the faces sticking together. Every fourteen days the engine and transmission should be rotated, the engine can be turned with the handle and the transmission by turning one of the back wheels since these will be jacked off the ground; one of the gears should be in mesh.

The Chassis

The chassis should be well cleaned and then lubricated, any rust spots that are noticed should be touched up to prevent the damage from spreading. The handbrake should be left in the "off" position. Jack up all the wheels, keep the tires inflated and covered up from the light which is injurious to rubber when in store.

Keep the whole car covered with a full-length dust sheet as dust contains many chemicals which are injurious to both the paintwork and the bright parts. Occasionally remove the dust sheet and give the whole car a general inspection, and if there are any signs of bloom formation remove it by repolishing at once. On no account be tempted to start the engine during storage as this will leave condensation inside the cold engine which will lead to corrosion.

If you have to lay-up your car under circumstances where you will be unable to visit it periodically it is possible to buy a sheet of p.v.c. of sufficient size in which to wrap the whole car. After cleaning and generally preparing the car for storage as we have outlined above, remove the battery, lay the sheet of p.v.c. on the floor and push the car onto it. Place a bowl of silica-gel under the centre of the car and a dust sheet over the top to prevent the p.v.c. touching the paintwork to which it might stick in time. Then fold the p.v.c. over the top of the car and seal all the edges of the package by melting them together with a hot iron.

CHAPTER X

CLUBS

THERE is little doubt that a large part of the enjoyment derived from the pursuit of any hobby lies in the sharing of that enjoyment with other people. The ownership of a Vintage car is no exception to this rule and although one may burn a great deal of midnight oil in the solitary confines of the workshop or reel off many a mile of good Vintage motoring, none of this would be much fun if you did not know that sooner or later you could meet others of a like mind to yourself. It is also a great relief at times to be able to visit another man's workshop and to see that he has had to overcome similar problems to your own to keep his car on the road. Altogether there is a great social side to our pastime and very naturally certain clubs have been founded to bring together those of us with a common interest and to promote the enjoyable use of Vintage cars in various types of competition.

Membership of at least one club is really imperative if you are to enjoy using your car to the full and club membership will also bring with it considerable advantages which may not at first sight be apparent. For instance, by meeting people with a like motor-car to your own the ever-persistent problem of finding sources of spare parts can often be solved. Certain clubs extend facilities for overcoming any difficulties which you might have in connection with insurance. If you are thinking of owning a Vintage car for the first time it can be a considerable help to join a club before the purchase is made and to get the advice of other members on the desirability or otherwise of owning the particular make and model which you had in mind.

However, apart from all the side-benefits, the main function of the clubs is to bring together like-minded people and to organise social and competitive meetings for the members' enjoyment. The social events, which can range from a get-together at a pub for a drink and a natter to a film show or a lecture, are generally organised to take place during the winter months when motoring is at a low ebb. The competitive type of event which can be a race meeting, a rally with driving tests, a *concours d'élégance* or a trial, is generally held in the summer and at one of these some of the members will compete, others will help with the organisation of the event and the remainder will come to spectate, speculate and generally rattle on about the same old subjects of which one never seems to tire. There is no more pleasant way of spending a day than to attend a meeting of Vintage cars and their owners, where the great common interest is the motor-cars and such trivial differences as rank and wealth are completely forgotten.

Before giving a more detailed account of some of the clubs we must say that we feel, apart from the advantages of being a member, one is morally bound to support at least one club as there is no doubt had they not existed that no car of thirty or more years old would be allowed to run on the public roads today.

* * *

The Vintage Sports-Car Club

In 1934 a small band of enthusiasts found that they were often meeting each other at the Phoenix Green Garage at Hartley Wintney in Hampshire where motor-cars of the very best type made in the previous decade were bought, sold and repaired. The garage was well situated as it was next-door to the Phoenix Inn where these enthusiasts could get refreshment and continue their discussions about the fine cars of yesterday and bemoan the general lowering of standards in the motor industry which they felt were currently taking place. They all considered that during the years 1919–1930 design had risen to a peak and that now it was rapidly falling away to an all-time low. They also felt that it would be a fine thing to encourage the preservation of the best of the cars of those Vintage years and in particular the cars with high performance and handling qualities. Their common interest led to the formation of the Vintage Sports-Car Club and, although it is always difficult to mention names without leaving out some of the most deserving, those who were among the founder members and who are still prominent in the club today are Cecil Clutton, Tim Carson, Tom Rolt, and Harry Bowler. Sammy Davis and the late Forrest Lycett were also keen early members.

We do not propose to write a potted history of the Vintage Sports-Car Club but only to say briefly what it does for its members today. From such a small beginning in 1934 it has grown to an internationally famous institution with over four thousand members. The only qualification for full membership is that you own a car made before 1931 and that you have a recommendation from two other members of the club. You can be a driving member by owning one of certain specified makes and models made between 1931 and 1939, known as Post Vintage Thoroughbreds, or an Historic Racing Car which must be a genuine racing car at least twelve years old. If you do not own a qualifying car but wish to be a member then you can become an associate of the club but as such you can only compete in events if you can borrow an eligible car from another member. As the members are spread all over the country regional sections have been formed, each of which has its own committee elected by the regional members and each region organises its own events, in addition to the main events which are run by the headquarters staff of the club.

An excellent quarterly club magazine, the *Bulletin*, is sent to every member and keeps him in touch with club events and also contains erudite articles on Vintage motor-car history and not a little humour. The club has a full time secretary in Tim Carson whose untiring efforts, together with those of his wife Margery, have kept the very complex organisation of the club running smoothly for many years.

The Vintage Sports-Car Club organise three full-scale race meetings every year, a feature of each of these being one race for suitable cars of the Edwardian era. The race meetings also provide for Historic Racing Cars and have thus encouraged the preservation of many interesting and exciting machines which would otherwise have been purely static museum pieces. The majority of the racing is naturally for Vintage and P.V.T. cars and very large entries are always forthcoming for every race. Most of the races are from seven to twelve miles in length and due to a very highly developed form of handicapping a good chance of winning is open to all participants.

The club also holds an annual hill-climb at Prescott in Worcestershire, entry to which is restricted to Edwardian and Vintage cars. The Vintage Prescott meeting is one of the most pleasant and informal motoring events imaginable held in a particularly lovely setting. There is a full-scale rally held in the winter with about 200 miles of road section to be dealt with at night and throughout the year there are innumerable trials, rallies, driving tests, *concours d'élégance* and purely social meetings organised by the various sections.

We think that we have said enough about the Vintage Sports-Car Club to indicate that if you have a car and are a member you need never have a dull moment and in addition you can insure your car through the club scheme provided that it is in a sound and roadworthy condition. The annual subscription is thirty shillings, and in addition to all the other services a monthly list of members' cars for sale and wanted is published. The club has a lending library of manuals and instruction books and there is also a spares registrar.

The Bentley Drivers' Club

Of all the many clubs which limit their membership to the owners of one make of car the Bentley Drivers' Club is probably the best known. Originally founded in 1936 for the benefit of those interested in owning and using the cars made by the original Bentley Company the club has since enlarged its scope to cover owners of all models bearing the name Bentley regardless of age. It so happens that the demise of the original company nearly coincided with what has now become known as the end of the Vintage era and so all cars made by them are considered to qualify as Vintage Cars by the V.S.C.C. Membership qualifications are that you own a Bentley car and that you are sponsored by two existing members but, once you have joined, a temporary loss of the Bentley-owning status does not disqualify you from continued membership.

Although naturally not so large as the V.S.C.C. the club produces a very fine quarterly magazine, known as the *Review*, which forms a continuous record of the activities of club members and also contains articles of technical and historic interest to owners of Bentley cars. Membership is scattered all over the world, but in the United Kingdom it is divided into geographical regions, each of which has its own committee to organise local events of all types. The main club events each year consist of a race meeting, a hill climb, a rally, a *concours d'élégance*, driving tests and an annual dinner and dance. The club has been responsible for the production of a very comprehensive instruction manual covering all Vintage models of Bentley which is available to members and in addition the members themselves have naturally acquired a wealth of technical information which is passed on by word of mouth.

Again it is difficult to mention names without leaving out many who well deserve great praise for their work in building up the club, but the name of Stanley Sedgwick is synonymous with the B.D.C. Originally the secretary, and now the very hard-working president, he is ably backed by an equally diligent committee. The immediate past secretary, Darrel Berthon, now an executive vice-president, also put many years of sweat and toil into bringing the club to its present eminence.

The annual subscription is two guineas and a monthly advertiser is published telling of members' cars for sale or wanted.

The Bullnose Morris Club

When one considers that a bullnose Morris, which went out of production in 1926, could be bought for as little as £5 in 1931 it is somewhat surprising that enough of them still existed in 1952 for a club to be formed to encourage their preservation. Such, however, was the case and Egerton Ferguson, who founded the club, has been proved right in thinking that sufficient people would share his views and that the club would prosper. There are now nearly three hundred pre-1926 cars registered with the club which has also opened its membership to those who, although not actually owning a bullnose Morris, are sufficiently interested in their preservation to support the club's activities. The owner of a bullnose M.G., an early Morris derivative, is also welcomed to the club.

Membership brings with it the services of the spares registrar R. M. Knox, whose efforts in locating sources of spare parts, some of which are still available through the maker's normal channels, have seen to it that no early Morris need be off the road through a lack of the vital part.

The club organises one or two main rallies each year and in addition members are invited to participate in many events of other one-make clubs which, due to small membership, welcome the additional cars at their events.

No description of the Bullnose Club would be complete without a mention of the name of Lytton Jarmon who has tirelessly gathered together the early history of this make of car and has accumulated probably one of the most complete technical records in existence specialising in just one manufacturer. As well as being the club librarian he assists R. I. Barraclough in the production of a quarterly club magazine which is circulated to all members. Possibly due to this very complete technical record of the Morris the club places a high premium on originality of specification in their marking at *concours*, even down to the shades of colour which were available when the cars were new.

The annual subscription is one pound.

The Alvis Register

In 1948 Bob Burgess and Paul Guiggin decided that there was a sufficient number of enthusiastic owners of vintage Alvis cars to merit the formation of a register. In the case of Alvis the V.S.C.C. deadline of December 1930 as the end of the Vintage period cuts across the production of certain models which continued until the Motor Show of 1932. The Alvis Register has therefore sensibly catered for all owners of cars made up until this date although their decision to do so does not make the 1931–32 cars Vintage in the normally recognised meaning of the word.

The present registrar is Norman Johnson whose energetic efforts since 1952 have built up the membership by providing an organisation which enables owners of similar cars to keep in touch with one another. This organisation provides technical information on all models from the commencement of manufacture until 1932 and also holds occasional rallies and social meetings. A monthly circular in addition to a quarterly bulletin is issued to all members and both of these publications contain news of members' activities, articles of technical interest and announcements of members' cars for sale or wanted. The production of all this wealth of information has been the task of Derek Preston for many years.

It may come as a surprise to many readers that over eight hundred pre-1933 Alvis cars are known by the Register to exist and a very high proportion of this number are still in regular use. The Register places great importance on the fact that most of the members use their cars regularly as normal transport, and that they are able to do so is in large part due to the efforts of George Putman who keeps them advised on sources of spare parts where the makers are now unable to supply. It must be said that Messrs. Alvis Limited take a great interest in any car which they have made, however old it may be, and can still help with certain spares.

Alvis Register members can compete in Inter-Register Club competitive events and the annual subscription is one pound.

The 20-Ghost Club

As the name implies this is a club for owners of Rolls-Royce cars, the name being made up from the titles of two of the models made during the Vintage period.

Formed in 1950, the club's simply stated aim was to foster the social gathering of persons interested in Rolls-Royce cars built prior to 31st December 1939. Although since that time the social gatherings have on occasion become competitive the club still remains essentially a promoter of family gatherings in pleasant surroundings where owners may compare their cars, if they wish, and their families may spend a happy day in the gardens of some country estate or other typically English scene. This is exactly as it should be; the Rolls-Royce is not a car to be flung round driving tests or thrown up a hill climb but is at its best pushing back the miles early on a summer's morning in its effortless way heading towards the rendezvous away from the madding crowd. Nothing can look finer than a smartly turned out Forty-Fifty tourer standing, perhaps, in a paddock in the grounds of a country house and in such a setting twenty or thirty such cars can give their owners plenty of scope for a full day's enthusiastic natter. Finally the drive home at night, after a good meal at a country pub, allowing plenty of time for all the Jones's to get home first, finishes off a perfect day in which the car has played its full part like a perfect servant, never intruding but always at the ready.

Certain meetings of the 20-Ghost Club include driving tests, *concours d'élégance* and *concours d'état*. There is a quarterly magazine called the *20-Ghost Club Record*, a well illustrated publication containing accounts of club events and a small number of technical articles. The club does not have any technical information service officially laid-on, but naturally there is a wealth of such knowledge held amongst the members and by meeting and getting to know them one need not be without any piece of Rolls-Royce lore for very long.

Membership is open to owners of any pre-1940 model of Rolls-Royce but members of the motor trade are not eligible as a general principle of the club. The annual subscription is two guineas.

The 20-Ghost Club were responsible, in 1962, together with the help of the Rolls-Royce Enthusiasts Club, the Rolls-Royce Section of the Vintage Sports-Car Club, the Midland Rolls-Royce Club and the Bentley Drivers Club, for what was certainly the most fabulous gathering of cars of one make which has ever been held. By issuing an invitation to any Rolls-Royce owner to forgather at Blenheim Palace on a certain Sunday morning they achieved the fine sight of about seven hundred of the well known radiators in row upon row in a perfect English setting and, as an aside, they asked the owners of Bentleys to come, too, which added another three hundred to the throng. The effect of this upon certain overseas visitors who had been invited as guests was very satisfying.

The man whose name will always be coupled with the 20-Ghost Club is Stanley Sears, their president, who has a large collection of the most desirable Rolls-Royce cars, all of which are turned out in impeccable state. Fred Watson has been the honorary club secretary since its inception and he not only turns up to meetings in a very fine pre-1914 Ghost but also sees to it that all the members feel thoroughly at home.

The Aston Martin Owners' Club

The output per week of Aston Martin cars has never been measured in hundreds nor even in dozens over the whole history of the marque but we suppose that it would be fair to say that a higher proportion of the total output is still on the road than of any other make which has been in production for around forty years. The Aston Martin has always been a sports-car and the club therefore has a strong bias towards sporting events, particularly race meetings of which it holds three each year. The membership of the club is composed of full members, who have to be current owners of an Aston Martin, and associate members, who are deemed sufficiently keenly interested in the make by two existing full members to be proposed by them. Naturally, club events cater for members owning cars from the beginning of the name right up to the present day so that one can not only see some historic cars performing as they did long ago but also the very latest in Gran Turismo and sports-racing cars in action.

Membership will cost you two guineas a year for which you get, in addition to competitive and social events, a monthly magazine and a technical information service should you need it.

Aston Martin ownership is spread all over the world and the club has many overseas members and is probably unique in the fact that it has several overseas owners on its main committee to represent those who cannot join in the general activities of the club but to whom membership is a very definite link with home.

The Alvis Owner Club

While the Alvis Register limits its membership to cars of that make made up until late 1931 the Alvis Owner Club caters for models of any date. However, those who have the Vintage models tend to belong to the Register as it specialises in their particular era. The Alvis Owner Club runs one very famous event each year known as National Alvis Day which is held at the Crystal Palace and which is probably the largest gathering of one make of car to be held annually as a normal club fixture. A very good technical service is run by the club, covering all models of Alvis made from 1932 onwards and a spares registrar can give details of likely sources of supply for replacement parts on the older cars when these are not now available from the makers. In passing we should say that

Alvis Limited have a very fine reputation for being able to supply a great number of the spares for pre-war models, but there are bound to be certain items which it would be impossible for any manufacturer to stock against a very small demand and it is to fill this gap that the spares registrar exists.

The annual subscription is two guineas a year and the only condition of joining the club is that you own an Alvis car. A monthly magazine called the *Bulletin* is sent to all members. The club is divided into geographical sections, each with its own committee who arrange social and competitive events to suit the members in their areas.

The S.T.D. Register and Club

The initials in the title of this club stand for three famous names in motoring history, Sunbeam, Talbot and Darracq. Considering the international fame which these three names acquired during the Vintage period it is very surprising how few of their products exist today. Somehow their ranks suffered more than most during the 'thirties and the war period so that by the time Mrs. Winifred Boddy, wife of W. Boddy, the editor of *Motor Sport*, decided to gather together those owners who were still lovingly tending and using cars of these makes, they were fairly thin on the ground. However, due to her action in 1950 the rot was stopped and today the Register which she founded has grown to include the name club in its title, has a full committee to run it and issues a bi-monthly magazine called *Sunbeam*.

Like most one-make clubs it has one annual event for which it is known to outsiders as well as several smaller events which do not receive as much publicity. In the case of the S.T.D. Register and Club the yearly pilgrimage to the birthplace of the Sunbeam car, Wolverhampton, is quite famous and all the members who possibly can manage it take their cars back to the works where they were made. In addition there are driving tests, *concours d'élégance* and social meetings held during the year.

Membership is open to all who own one of the specified makes of car made before 1936, which marked the end of the original companies, and costs one pound each year. A spares register and technical information service is run by the club and Mrs. Boddy has now handed over her executive duties to various committee members but remains the president.

The Humber Register

The founders of the Humber Register fully agreed with those of the Vintage Sports-Car Club in that they felt that the bottom went out of motor-car design at the end of 1930. They limit full membership of their register to owners of Humber cars made before 1931 although they rather grudgingly admit owners of cars made before 1939 as associate members hoping, probably. that by contact with the earlier models they may eventually see the light and make themselves eligible for full membership.

Specialising as they do in what was an exceedingly well made touring car with no sporting attributes whatsoever, the events run by this register tend to be social rather than competitive, but they have fostered among their members a keen spirit of always producing their cars in a clean and original state which might well be a little more accentuated by certain other clubs. No matter how much one enjoys the driving there is really no excuse for coming out in public with an unkempt motor-car and you will seldom see a Humber that is not presentable.

The Humber Register was formed in 1951, produces a bi-monthly magazine for members edited by A. B. Demaus to whom the register owes its formation, runs a technical service and a spares register. They also have a library from which technical books on the various models can be borrowed and can help members to insure their cars at reasonable rates. Their big annual meeting is the rally at Thame in Oxfordshire. Other rallies and competitions are run in conjunction with other registers throughout the summer season. The annual subscription is one pound.

The Lagonda Club

Unlike many makes of motor-car we think it true to say that the Lagonda gradually improved from its inception right up until the outbreak of war, suffering no particular set-back in design at the end of the Vintage period. The Lagonda Club, which is an amalgamation of two very much older clubs, the Lagonda Car Club and the 2-litre Register, was formed in 1951 and has no deadlines of date. Membership depends entirely on being sincerely interested in, or owning, a Lagonda car. The club runs a number of events each year to suit various tastes and these include driving tests, navigational rallies, *concours d'élégance* and an annual sprint meeting. Similarly to the owners of Alvis cars most Lagonda owners use their cars as every day transport because, having a reasonable performance, they have no difficulty in keeping up with modern traffic and the club therefore puts considerable emphasis on giving the members a good technical information service and guide to sources of spares.

An illustrated quarterly magazine is sent to all members who pay one and a half guineas a year to belong to the club.

The Bugatti Owners' Club

Founded in 1929 the Bugatti Owners' Club is most famous for its ownership of Prescott Hill in Worcestershire, probably the most picturesque setting for any motoring event held in this country. Originally the club was only open to owners of Bugatti cars but now it is open to anyone who is proposed and seconded by existing members. When the club was founded the marque was at the zenith of its racing career and it has therefore inherited the traditions direct from Molsheim, whereas other clubs have had painstakingly to search back through history to pick up the threads of makes now long defunct.

A quarterly illustrated magazine called *Bugantics* records the club's activities and gives owners both historical and technical information about their cars. In addition the club has a technical consultant whose services will be invaluable if you decide to own a Bugatti as this particular make of car runs to many different types, some of which have very individual engineering features that are easily deranged if they are not properly understood. The Bugatti racing cars are delightful pieces of mechanical craftsmanship and if your leaning is towards the ownership of a watch-like mechanism of high potency then one of these is just what you want. The Bugatti Owners' Club will be a great help to you with advice on its maintenance and will also provide you with several hill climbs each year in which to use it.

Contrary to popular belief the sports and touring models of Bugatti are very reliable if looked after properly and are famed for their precision handling qualities.

The annual subscription is three guineas a year.

* * *

We have by no means mentioned all the clubs and registers who specialise in looking after the owners of Vintage and Thoroughbred cars and we must apologise to all those who have been left out, and also for the omission of the names of deserving people who have laboured mightily in the cause of some of the clubs which we have mentioned. A full list of clubs and registers appears in Appendix II. Really the purpose of this chapter has been to give what we think is a representational cross section of the amenities that exist to help anyone who owns a car made between the wars, and to show a reader who might be wondering if he could cope with this strange hobby of ours that he need not feel alone in the world but that by joining the right club, or clubs, he will certainly find all the help and good fellowship that he wants.

CHAPTER XI

USE OF THE CAR IN RALLIES AND DRIVING TESTS

If you are proposing to compete in rallies or driving tests this chapter is for your guidance in choosing the most suitable events and outlines the paper work necessary before you can enter, the special equipment required, the preparation of the motor-car and also gives hints and tips on the actual running. Since neither of the authors has had much experience of this form of competition we have collected the information from our old friend Michael Usher, who has considerable knowledge of driving in these types of event. Before we pass on to the gen there is one point we should like to stress. Rallies are becoming a little unpopular with the public and the police, and since it is necessary for them to be held on the public roads if there is to be continuity of this form of competition then it behoves the crews to take care that the driving is within the law, that other road users are not inconvenienced and, if the rally is at night, that people living in the districts on the rally route who are hoping to sleep are not disturbed by unnecessary noise.

We presume that anyone considering competing in a rally will be a competent road driver, this is certainly necessary as he will probably need to do some fairly fast driving possibly on tricky roads in bad weather conditions.

If you have no experience of either rallies or driving tests it might be a good thing to get in touch with your nearest well known Motor Club and enquire if they run courses of instruction on both these branches of the sport, many of the leading clubs do this and they are only too eager to assist keen newcomers.

Paperwork

Before you enter for any event the driver will need to have a currently valid driving licence appropriate to the class of vehicle; he will also require a Competition Licence, this must be obtained from the Royal Automobile Club, price 15s., or a Club Membership Card if it is a closed competition. You should get a copy of the R.A.C. Motor Sport Year Book and Fixture List for the current year, price 2s. 6d., which will give you the Standing Supplementary Regulations for rallies and driving test meetings and you should also have a copy of the Vintage Sports-Car Club Eligibility Regulations.

Having decided to enter and found what you think is a suitable event you must next send to the Secretary of the meeting for an entry form and a copy of the Supplementary Regulations; not only will you have to state the particulars of the car to be used but you will probably have to nominate your navigator as he may qualify for a separate award.

Choice of Crew

It is essential if you are to have any hope of success that you have a competent navigator who is calm and confident and in whom you can place the utmost trust. He, or she, must have complete faith in you as there is no time for the slightest difference of opinion. It must be clearly understood from the start that successful rallying is all a matter of team work.

The navigator must plot the route and then direct the driver with clear instructions. He should give sufficient directions to enable the driver to proceed to a given point and while the driver is carrying out those instructions the navigator should thus be in a position to continue plotting the route on the map, so that when the driver has reached the given point the navigator can give continuity of instruction for the next section of the route without any loss of time. It should be decided beforehand which member of the crew is to be responsible for time-keeping as this is just as essential as route finding. At this point it is worth considering if any advantage will be obtained by having a third member for the crew whose sole responsibility is time-keeping and presentation of the route card or road book at controls, and who in an emergency can take the place of the navigator. It should be remembered that even the most experienced navigator can be smitten with bouts of nausea due to concentration on his maps and for a period be completely incapacitated. The admitted advantage of a team of more than two should be considered in relation to the space and power available in the car. For instance, four bods in an Austin Seven would be rather cramped and much too heavy. A third member is certainly a great advantage if the route includes gated roads as his responsibility can be the opening and closing of the gates but it is essential that he is able to leave the car without disturbing the driver or navigator. If there is not to be a third member for the team the onus of opening and closing gates must rest with the navigator and care must be taken on such occasions before leaving the car to stow away all the documents. It is very annoying and it could be a major disaster to have to retrace the route against a flow of other competitors for about five miles to retrieve that road book from the mud at the last gate.

Clothing

It is extremely difficult to lay down any hard and fast rules for suitable clothing as it is largely a matter of personal taste but in any case clothing for rallies should be warm and light in weight and it must be so designed that it cannot restrict the use of controls or impede the inevitable calls of nature at a time when the fingers may be somewhat numb. Suitable clothing is stocked by those firms who specialise in equipment for motor sport. For driving tests warm clothing is not so important since the periods of driving are so short, the emphasis in this case should be on light weight and easy fitting so that the use of controls is in no way restricted. The clothing should have no looseness to get caught in parts of the car—trousers for instance may be tucked into the socks.

Preparation of the Car

Your car should be in good mechanical condition. Check that the brakes are sound and that the linings are not down to the rivets, adjust them carefully so that when the brakes are applied the car will pull up all square on a wet road. Examine the steering and see that it is well lubricated and also make sure that the shock absorbers are efficient and properly adjusted. The tires must be in good condition, likewise the entire electrical system if you are entered for a night rally. If you have any doubts about the sparking plugs it is a good investment to fit a new set: inspect the whole car to make certain that everything is secure and this includes the contents. Spares, however desirable, are not an asset if they can roll about the driving compartment and possibly become jammed in the gear-lever gate, or even worse lodged under the brake pedal. The practice of carrying competition numbers is now dying out but if these are specified it is far better to have proper plates to carry them, securely fixed at the front and at the rear of the car with some suitable device for holding the card in place, such as rubber bands. The alternative of attaching the number cards to the car with Sellotape is neither tidy nor is it very efficient. It is considered to be very bad form to leave in position any competition numbers after the completion of the event and this clause is usually found to be specified in the supplementary regulations.

Spares and Equipment

If you think that certain spares may be required, by all means carry them, but do not overload the car with unnecessary junk as this will upset the power-to-weight ratio and also cause discomfort to the crew. The following is a list of bits and pieces that are necessary. A jack, wheel brace spanner or copper hammer depending on the type of wheels fitted to your car, insulating tape, a coil of soft copper wire and an assortment of nuts and bolts are useful. A tow rope, a tire pressure gauge and a good pump should be carried as you may need to vary the tire pressures to suit road conditions. The organisers of night rallies usually arrange facilities for you to obtain petrol on the route but you might break down and never get to the filling station so it is advisable to carry with you a spare two gallon can of petrol. Do not however, pack this alongside your food—petrol fumes do not improve the flavour of caviare sandwiches. If the rally is at night the car should be fitted with fog lamps and a reversing lamp and another useful piece of equipment for illumination is a Helphos search-light and handlamp; this accessory is intended for attachment to the windscreen but it will be found that it is far better to have it loose, but of course plugged into the battery, as it is then more easily swung round to point in any direction. Carry some spare bulbs and a good torch and always have a first aid kit with you.

Navigational Equipment

It is usually necessary for you to provide the 1-inch Ordnance Survey Maps, 7th series, specified in the supplementary regulations for the particular rally in which you have entered. Paper maps are recommended as not only are these very much less expensive than the cloth variety but they are far more handy to use in the car due to their much greater ease of folding. A map-board and clips are very useful and you will require pencils or ball point pens, a good quality perspex rule, a pair of dividers, a magnetic compass and an opisometer. For night work an illuminated magnifying glass is absolutely essential. The time-keeper will require a reliable watch and a board for his papers; the board and watch must have some form of illumination at night. In some rallies the organisers specify the use of sealed watches but in this case they will be supplied. An essential piece of equipment is a set of average speed tables or a calculator. If you become a very keen participant in rallies there is a wide range of equipment available but it is much better to wait until you have gained sufficient experience to judge just what extra equipment you will require. Before you turn up for your first rally make sure that you have a dummy run in the car to be used and with your crew and the equipment, so that you can get things sorted out before the actual day. Two hours is quite sufficient for this purpose but the run should be carried out in the same conditions, that is day or night, as the rally for which you have entered.

If you have fitted any new electric lighting, either exterior or interior, test it on the road at night to be sure that it will give the required illumination and without causing any dazzle.

Should you pass through a water splash during the rally be sure to dry out your brakes by repeated application as soon as possible afterwards as otherwise you may find yourself in an emergency without any power of retardation.

If food and drink is to be carried it is better to confine this to boiled sweets and a vacuum flask of coffee or hot soup; a good alternative would be chocolate and fruit.

Be sure to turn up at the venue of the meeting with plenty of time in hand so that you can check the car and the equipment at your leisure; there is nothing worse than to present yourself to the starter all hot and bothered and out of breath. At no time must you question the validity of your navigator's decision—put your tongue in your cheek and follow his direction without hesitation, and the satisfaction of arriving at the next control having been told to turn right at the last fork where the two preceding competitors turned left will make you realise that your crew have some clues in their particular sphere. If possible never baulk other competitors: if you have a faster car behind you then let him through as soon as possible; treat all marshals with respect and never argue with them, remember that they are giving up their time and working very hard so that you and the other competitors can have the pleasure of competing in the event.

If you should have the misfortune to be forced to retire do have the courtesy to inform the organisers of the rally, otherwise they may think that you are stranded on the top of Snowdon or possibly at the bottom of Lake Vyrnwy, and have to send out a search party.

We hope that this information will help you on your way to become a successful rallyist.

VIII RALLYING A VINTAGE CAR: *Cecil Clutton, a past president of the Vintage Sports-Car Club, taking part in a rally in his 1928 Type 44 Bugatti*

IX RACING A VINTAGE CAR: *Nigel Arnold-Forster racing his 1922 5,136 c.c. Delage during a Vintage Sports-Car Club race meeting at Oulton Park*

CHAPTER XII

USE OF THE CAR IN RACES AND SPEED EVENTS

It goes without saying that there are some Vintage motor-cars which are more suitable for racing than others but the art of handicapping has been so well developed in this country that if you are keen to try your hand round a circuit, no matter what make of car you own, provided that it is in good order, you will have an equal chance with everyone else in a handicap race. Scratch racing is for the more experienced and the faster types of car but let us hope that if your appetite is whetted after your first few handicap races you will graduate to the sterner field where everyone starts together and there is no doubt that the best combination of car and man wins.

Before continuing with this chapter we must make the admission that neither of us has ever graduated from the spectator class at speed events, so that all the practical information given herein has been gleaned from our great friend Gordon McDonald, who has done probably as much racing with a Vintage car as anyone in the world.

Paperwork

Before you can start racing there are certain items of paperwork which have to be gathered together; some of these need to be studied fairly carefully. The first is a copy of the Standing Supplementary Regulations of the R.A.C. which can be obtained from the Secretary, The Competitions Department, Royal Automobile Club, Pall Mall, London. S.W.1., price 2s. 6d. They contain all the regulations covering all types of motorsporting events held in this country and it is very important to read and to digest those which will apply to your particular form of competition.

The next document required is a Competition Licence. Again this is obtainable only from the R.A.C. and is necessary for all events excepting those which are restricted purely to members of the club concerned. In the latter case one's club membership card acts in lieu of a competition licence. In order to obtain a competition licence you must be the holder of a current driving licence and must have passed your driving test. Together with your competition licence you will receive a Medical Certificate form which must be filled in by your doctor and which, like the licence, is renewable annually.

Lastly, it is advisable to obtain from the Secretary of the V.S.C.C. a copy of the Eligibility of Cars leaflet which gives details of period classification, type classification and allowable modifications in respect of pre-1939 cars for V.S.C.C. events and which is accepted as the gospel for most clubs running events for such cars.

Personal Equipment

Until quite recently it was possible to go racing in a deerstalker hat if you felt so inclined, but this is now frowned upon by the R.A.C. and rightly so too. You must have a crash helmet and we advise that you get one of the motor-car type with a peak so that you can wear a vizor if you so desire. There are many good makes on the market but do see that the one you choose bears the British Standards approval mark which ensures a certain minimum standard of construction. To go with this helmet you can either have goggles or a vizor but as the vizor gives a far larger field of vision and is very much less subject to steaming up than goggles, and also does not need nearly so much wiping if it rains, we strongly advise trying the vizor. It is very advisable to wear gloves when racing, which can be hot work and can lead to slippery conditions on the wheel from sweating palms. Gloves will also protect your hands in the event of fire or your falling out onto the track. Thin leather gloves are vastly superior to any other type.

Your shoes should be as narrow as possible with no projecting welt to catch under pedals and should have leather soles which provide the maximum grip when wet. Normal clothes can be worn but these must be capable of being securely fastened and must not flap in the wind. Remember that it may quite easily be raining and an ordinary macintosh will probably end up wrapped round the gear lever at the most inopportune moment. A waterproof golf jacket is the best dress in rain; if it is fine a pullover and flannel trousers which are tucked into your socks are as good as anything. Both these items should be made of pure wool which is fireproof.

Type of Race for Beginners

Probably the finest experience for a beginner is the One Hour High Speed Trial held twice each year by the V.S.C.C. at their Silverstone meetings. Here there is no winner; you are merely expected to complete a given number of laps in an hour to collect an award. You thus get plenty of time to settle down and to see how your performance compares with that of other people in similar cars to your own. It is, in fact, like a very long practice session and you have no need to press your car any harder than you wish.

Following this exercise you can enter for, say, two handicap races at the next meeting and you would do well to choose a pair which have a fair interval of time between them, if this is possible, because you may need time for adjustments in between. Limit yourself to 5- or 10-lap handicap races in the first season and see how you and your car stand up to these before going on to better things.

After the first few meetings you will know enough about what suits you to go your own way but, before ending this section, we would like to say that the other two forms of speed event will teach you very little about circuit racing, the sprint being something you can practise on any straight piece of road near to your home and the hill climb being an entirely specialised form of driving usually performed on a very narrow road. Both the latter can be very good fun and hill climbing calls for precision driving of a very high order.

Having decided where you want to make a start, apply for an entry and study the regulations which will be sent to you by the club concerned.

Preparation of Car

The most important fact to remember when preparing your car for a race is that it is a far better thing to finish the race and to be able to drive home than to have one brief moment of glory in the first lap and then to be towed away with a gaping hole in the side of the crankcase. Therefore start by giving your car a normal good maintenance check from end to end looking for anything that is coming loose and rectifying any faults which you find. A very searching way of doing this is to set about cleaning the whole car meticulously including the engine and all the chassis as this will ensure that at least you will have looked at all the parts carefully. Having done this you can then pay particular attention to the following points which will differ from normal maintenance.

The steering gear should have a special inspection for freedom of movement and lack of play in the moving parts. The brake linings should be inspected unless you know positively that there is plenty of lining left and, of course, the brakes should be adjusted up as closely as possible to give you the maximum life before the pedal reaches the floor board. Remember that the drums are going to get far hotter than normal and will therefore expand and let the pedal down for part of its travel regardless of lining wear. Inspect the tires, which should be in first-class order. The fifty miles or so which you will do in the hour speed trial is about the equivalent of 1,000 miles on the road for tire wear and you can judge whether you have sufficient tread left from this yardstick. For racing in the dry pressures should be raised 5–10 lb. p.s.i., in the wet use normal pressures.

If you have any doubts about the cooling system when you are motoring normally then you will surely be in trouble on the track. The number of cars one sees retiring enveloped in steam proves this and it will pay to have the radiator flow tested and rectified if necessary at your local radiator repair depot. Check all the coolant hoses, and if they look at all perished, change them. Sparking plugs also have a hard time when the engine is continually run up to full power and a new set will be a good insurance against misfiring.

See that all the floor boards are properly fixed down or you will find them rising in the wind which can be very embarrassing.

Also ensure that the hood is firmly lashed down. Do not try to do any last-minute so-called tuning of the engine as this will probably make it far less reliable than it was before.

A fire extinguisher fitted within easy reach from the driving seat is a very worthwhile addition to the car and, once you have fitted it, do not remove it after the race because you might just as easily want it on the road. A tap in the main fuel line within the cockpit is also a good precautionary modification, particularly if you have a pressure feed from the tank. If you have a gravity tank you must have such a tap.

Lastly, change the engine oil the day before the meeting and remove from the car any impedimenta which you will not need at the race meeting —that map of Northern Ireland from under the driving seat for instance.

You can now load the car up with a certain amount of gear which will be useful to you at the meeting and which will prevent you depending upon other competitors who have been more thoughful than you. First, a really good tool kit in a separate bag that can be left in the paddock. We shall not outline what this should contain because so much depends upon your type of car but the more comprehensive it is the less likely are you to be stuck. In addition to tools we will mention a tow rope, a piece of chalk with which to write "On Tow" and some rubber tube of a suitable diameter to mend a broken fuel or oil pipe. A very small additional kit, which can be left in the car, containing an adjustable spanner, a pair of pliers, a screwdriver, some copper wire and a small roll of insulating tape or Scotch brand Electrical Tape No. 33, can be very useful if you break down half way round the circuit. This kit must be securely located in the car.

Finally, if you do not want to have your racing numbers painted on the car at the track you can either paint them on detachable discs for either side of the car and on a small plate for the front if front numbers are required, or they can be cut from cardboard, either black or white depending upon the colour of the car, and fixed to the car at the meeting with self-adhesive plastic tape. It is not at all the done thing to travel to or from the meeting with your racing numbers in place.

Get everything ready in plenty of time before the meeting and start in time on the day to get there early. Nothing will spoil your pleasure more than arriving hot under the collar at the last moment.

On Arrival at the Meeting

When you get to the meeting drive straight to the paddock and park your car in the place allotted to you. This will be your piece of ground for the rest of the day and you will only be in someone's way if you park anywhere else. Go immediately to race control and sign in so that the organisers will know that you are present. The next job is to prepare your car for scrutiny and practice and all surplus equipment should be unloaded from the car first. You can now remove any parts of the car which you are allowed by the regulations to be without while racing. This will largely depend on how seriously you feel about making the car go as well as possible, but you should certainly remove the spare wheel and make finally certain that there are no loose pieces inside the car. If the headlamps are left on the car the glasses will have to be taped over with insulating tape or surgical plaster. Fit your racing numbers in place, check your tire pressures and see that you have sufficient fuel, oil and water. When the car is fully prepared present yourself and the car for scrutiny seeing that you have your crash helmet, goggles or vizor, medical certificate and competition licence at the ready to show to the scrutineer.

The scrutineer is only concerned with the safety aspects of the car and is not the slightest bit interested in whether or not your car is likely to win the race, but a willing and agreeable demeanour and a clean motor-car can tend to incline him in your favour. Never argue with the scrutineer; he has generally got a great deal to do in a very short time and his word is law in any case. He will be chiefly concerned with the condition of your tires, the tightness of the wheel spokes, play in the king-pins, the condition of the steering connections and the backlash in the steering box. He will also inspect all the brake connections, the suspension attachments and the general security of all accessories. On the engine he will look for the provision of two return springs on the throttle control mechanism, so arranged that in the advent of the linkage falling to pieces, the butterflies will always return to the shut position. Any large oil leaks apparent on the engine may result in the scrutineer turning the car down in the interests of other people's safety.

Practice

Just before you go out onto the track for practice run over in your mind the meanings of the various flags which the flag marshals may wave at you and finally remember that you are going to drive on the right-hand side of the road. Set off on your first lap driving as though you were on a brisk main road run and merely relieved of the worry of people coming in the opposite direction. You will probably have time for an ample number of practice laps so take it steadily for the first few, keeping a constant watch in the mirror for faster cars when you pull into the centre of the road approaching corners. The golden rule about cornering is that once you have placed the car on what you think is the proper line for entering the corner you can then put all your concentration on what is in front of you. The corner is yours by common consent and it is up to the man behind to steer round you if he wants to overtake in the corner. If you are doubtful about the line to take you will get a very good indication of the average opinion by the black line worn onto the road surface but if you are in a comparatively slow car you will save time by keeping to the inside of the bend. Once out of a corner it is again good manners to keep out of the way of the faster men by staying as near to the right as other people slower than yourself will allow.

Having to a certain extent settled down after a few laps you must start thinking about getting round a bit faster and also to give some consideration to the motor-car. It is a good idea to choose a convenient point on the circuit where you can glance at your oil pressure gauge and coolant thermometer once each lap—such as just after you have engaged top gear after leaving a corner and before you are getting ready for the next corner. It is very easy to overspeed your engine in the intermediate gears in the excitement of the moment and you will get round no faster for doing this. The ideal engine speed for changing up is when the next gear higher will bring the engine onto maximum torque but as this will probably be an unknown figure to you, a good rule is to run up to within a few hundred r.p.m. of the manufacturers' limit in each gear and then to change up. In the heat of the race you can use the lot if you feel so inclined but remember that you are only practising at present and that you do want to take part in the race proper.

If you have a friend who can time your laps and signal to you any improvement this is a great help. Work the speed up slowly and do not get led astray by other people who may or may not know what they are doing. A very good rule on corners is to enter slowly and to leave fast, always try to finish all your braking and gear changing before starting to turn the corner leaving only the steering on which to concentrate while rounding the bend. Speaking of gear changing, the novice is generally inclined to indulge in far too much of this which only wastes time. Each gear change will take a certain fraction of a second, however smoky you are with the stick and this means a few yards lost if it was unnecessary. If your lap times are being taken try going round for a lap or two in top gear except for very sharp corners and see what difference it makes.

Towards the end of the practice period try to compare your performance with those of others in similar cars and learn anything that you can from them without trying something silly—like following them into a corner at a very short distance apart determined to go round as fast as they do whatever happens. Your lap times should have now become fairly consistent and you should have noted the points before each corner where you have had to start braking to get round the corner on your line at your speed. You will find that these can be closed up as you gain experience but never use the brakes right to the limit to decide on your cut-off point because they will probably fade to a certain degree during the race and you want something up your sleeve to allow for this.

One last word of advice. If during practice or during the race anything odd seems to be happening to the car, slow down and pull into the paddock. There will be plenty more opportunities to race but pressing on with a sick engine is a mug's game and will probably cost you a lot of time and money as well as spoiling your day's fun.

The Race

Nearly everyone suffers from nerves before their first race, which is only natural, and it is well to have a simple drill worked out in your mind about the procedure on the starting grid. As you will probably be entered in a handicap race all the cars will not start together but there will be a good deal of noise around you and it is difficult to hear what your own engine is doing. Start the engine at the one minute signal and engage first gear with about thirty seconds to go. The starter's flag will be erect for approximately five seconds so when he raises it run your engine up to between one third and one half maximum revolutions and then concentrate on the flag. Immediately it starts to descend let in the clutch and accelerate away. If you are unlucky enough to be on a wet track beware of wheel spin and try very hard to concentrate on what you are doing and not to worry about other people for the first few yards. With most cars an early change into second gear pays off and after that you will carry on in the way you found best in the practising period.

Always drive within your own limitations and treat the first race as an extension of practice. Go as fast as you can without frightening yourself, but keep to the correct side of the track and out of the way of the faster men except actually in the corners. Excessive thrusting and passing slower cars on the wrong side is considered very selfish unless the slower car persists in keeping to the wrong side and remember that all this racing is for everybody's pleasure and not for yours alone.

If you are unfortunate enough to leave the track make certain that you are not endangering others when you rejoin the race. A day's enjoyment will be effectively marred for everyone present, in descending order, by death, injury or a broken motor-car.

When you have taken part in a season's racing you will find that all the information contained in this chapter will have become second nature to you and you will then either want to go on to better things or to give it up altogether but one thing is certain, you won't be in need of any more advice from us on the subject. Gordon McDonald sums up his dozen years of racing experiences in the following sentence:

"Going fast in a straight line is a crude pleasure, searing acceleration a little less crude but the most refined pleasure comes from cornering as fast and as neatly as your own car will permit."

Improving the Performance of the Car for Racing

We do not intend to write a treatise on the tuning of Vintage and

Thoroughbred Cars for racing purposes, a whole book could easily be devoted to the subject. In fact we rather deprecate the wholesale massacre of many very nice examples of real collectors' pieces that has gone on in past years in order to make what are really very second-class sports-racing cars. However, certain increases in performance can be gained in ways that do not detract from the original character of the car and in no way spoil its original appearance.

The most important single step that can be taken in this respect is weight reduction. Many cars have vast pieces of wrought ironwork built into them, often hidden, which can easily be replaced by more scientifically designed parts which are more satisfying to own than the original. The battery may be quite unnecessarily heavy; you don't need to run in a five-lap race with twenty-five gallons of petrol in the tank, and twin spare wheels and their mountings are a bit redundant in these days. It is important to watch the sprung to unsprung weight ratio when lightening the car and some front axle beams can lose a few pounds with a little judicious machining. The road holding of most cars is improved by lightening provided that the unsprung weight is reduced in proportion to the reductions made in the sprung weight.

The braking system is next in order of priority and in most cars this can be improved by starting again with new drums and seeing that the whole mechanism is in first class order.

Last in importance comes the power output of the engine and the methods of improving this are again a vast subject, but do remember that you are dealing with elderly machinery which is often irreplaceable, and remember also that the manufacturers were not necessarily fools when they decided on the power which their engine could give reliably without being in need of constant attention.

CHAPTER XIII

PREPARING FOR A CONCOURS

THERE are now quite a number of *concours d'élégance* meetings for Vintage and P.V.T. cars in this country, there are also some meetings on the Continent for which our cars are eligible and of course in America, but that is rather a long journey and in any case the standards there are incredibly high—they even check the water in the radiator for cleanliness. There is no doubt that competing in *concours* has done more than anything else to improve the general condition and appearance of Vintage and P.V.T. cars and for this reason alone it is a form of competition to be encouraged.

In the early days of motoring the *concours d'élégance* was a competition for new and usually costly motor-cars which were frequently posed together with an attractive and elegantly dressed female, and the judging was then purely on the elegance of the pair. The idea of having this member of the fair sex to accompany the car was presumably to catch the eye of the judge, usually male, by her voluptuous curves and so distract his attention from any fault in the contour of the motor-car body. The Vintage car *concours* as practised today should in most cases be termed a *concours d'état* since the aim is to judge the condition and cleanliness of the vehicle and so the female has been left out as obviously it would not be possible to include her in this type of inspection. This is all to the good as otherwise we might possibly have rather more judges than competitors.

The basis for marking differs from one meeting to another but marks are invariably awarded for the condition and cleanliness of the mudguards, wheels and the body both internally and externally and also under-bonnet and chassis cleanliness. Mechanical condition of both the engine and chassis are often part of the judging and at some meetings quite high marks are awarded for originality and yearly mileage, at others these are not considered at all. Marks may be awarded for comfort and elegance but in any case for most meetings the organisers state the basis for the marking in the supplementary regulations. Having decided on a *concours* for which you consider your car is suitable do make sure before you set off for the meeting that every part of your car is in as good a condition as possible and that it is absolutely clean in all details. Remember that if at the end of the judging there are two cars apparently faultless, then to decide a tie, the lights may be examined for ability to function, the dynamo for efficiency in charging or even the tool kit for condition. Never lubricate the chassis immediately before a *concours* as if you do you will probably find on arrival that your beautifully cleaned car has become smothered in oil and grease and that you have not the time available to clean it again. In any case, try to arrive with plenty of time in hand for that last minute polish and removal of smashed flies and also for the odd troubles that may have developed and require rectification.

If your route lies along country roads avoid patches of mud and to an even greater extent cow dung as this sets like concrete on a hot day and is very difficult to remove without lengthy soaking. Cleanliness is all a matter of hard work and it takes real labour and a long time if you are to have any hope of success at most meetings. It is no use just sending the car round to the local garage to have it cleaned; the judge will take in the well polished panels at the first glance and then start examining all the inaccessible nooks and corners in his search for old grime. Condition on the other hand will also probably entail hard work but it may, in addition, require the expenditure of some cash on a vehicle otherwise perfectly roadworthy and reliable. It all depends on how determined you are to have the perfect motor-car.

Mechanical Condition

Examine the engine, gear-box and rear axle for oil leaks. You may be required to run the engine and accordingly make sure that everything is in first class order so that it will start without undue delay and tick over evenly on all cylinders. Check the tappets if they are too audible, closing the gaps beyond the makers recommended clearance will not make them quiet but a loose tappet can nevertheless be noisy. Make sure that you have no leaks in the exhaust system and if necessary fit new gaskets and tighten up the joints. Examine the carburetter and the petrol system for leaks, also the radiator, the water pump and the rubber hoses. If the ignition leads are at all tatty then fit new ones. Be sure that the dynamo is charging correctly and that the starter motor is capable of rotating the engine with sufficient urge. The lamps should all be in working order and the battery capable of proving this fact. There should not be excessive play in the steering joints, the brake clevis pins, the king pins or the wheel hub bearings, and make sure that the brakes are properly adjusted so that the operating levers are at the correct angle.

Condition of Finish and Bodywork

The paintwork of your car may be in such good condition that in ordinary circumstances it looks very smart; you must remember however, that the judges will not take in the appearance of the car as a whole but they will be endeavouring to find blemishes in the less obvious places, such as round the edges of doors, mudguards and beadings. Examine the whole car thoroughly after it has been cleaned and if you find any defects these must be touched up with paint to match. If the fault is in the middle of a panel it may be necessary to repaint the entire area due to the difficulty of matching. With cellulose paint it is quite easy to fill in a blemish and then to polish it off to a perfect finish, but the colour of old paint will probably have changed with age and the new material may show up as a lighter spot when it is polished. A likely place to find trouble is round the mudguard fixings especially if you have domed headed bolts for holding the mudguards to the brackets. Unless these are absolutely tight cracking will occur in the paint round the edges. Dents must be removed or filled in. Mudguards must be clean inside, it is therefore advisable to clean the under surface, removing any hard mud or tar and then to paint them with a tough enamel in a matching colour. This may seem a lot of unnecessary hard work but remember that it will also prolong the life of the metal. If when you have cleaned the chassis and axles you find that the paint is chipped then these parts should be repainted but before doing so make sure that you have removed all the old encrustation of mud and grease. Nothing looks worse than paint applied on top of dirt, it is a mistake that shows up far more than some people seem to realise. We have often seen hexagon nuts and bolt heads glossy with enamel but with the appearance of being almost round. Plating must be in good condition so that if it has deteriorated you will have to remove the part and have it replated. Polished brass is sometimes seen on Vintage car fittings other than those under the bonnet, due to the nickel plating having been entirely removed by constant polishing; it is quite wrong to leave it like this. Marks will be lost by faulty plating or dents in the radiator shell but renovation of this part of the car can be an expensive job—the block will possibly have to be removed and the thin metal construction often does not take kindly to this treatment. At the worst a new block may be required, somewhat expensive if it is in a vee or curved form. Torn or frayed carpets and upholstery should be repaired unless you are going to replace them. Interior wood panelling can mar an otherwise smart motor-car if it is in a bad condition—such as veneer which is coming adrift due to rain water having penetrated underneath the surface. This should be repaired but it may be less expensive to replace it with solid hard wood of some suitable variety. If your car is an open model examine the hood frame and its mechanism and refinish it if this is necessary, also repair any faults in the hood fabric and tonneau cover and the press fasteners. At certain meetings you are given a choice of being judged on either the hood or tonneau cover. If you have a closed car examine the roof lining particularly round the edges of a sunshine roof when this is fitted.

Cleaning and Polishing

It is obvious that the cleaner and better polished your car is presented the better will be your chances of success, but many competitors do not realise that this means cleaning and polishing the more inaccessible places such as the edges of the doors, the back of the hinges, the foot pedals, the inside of the bonnet and behind brackets and fittings. It is often easier and more satisfactory to remove some of the fittings for cleaning particularly some of the plated parts.

The under-part of the car must be thoroughly clean and this does not mean just the chassis frame but also the axles and propeller shaft, the brake gear, the engine sump and gear box, the exhaust system and anything else that you can see when lying under the car. The engine should be cleaned down with petrol and for this purpose a one inch paint brush, a tooth brush and a test tube brush will be found most useful for reaching some of the more inaccessible places. Finish off with a rag, using a thin stick to insert small pieces of cleaning rag into the difficult spots. Brass, copper, plated parts and bright aluminium should be cleaned with metal polish and any chipped or rusty painted parts should be touched up. For black painted parts under the bonnet we have found that Llewellyn Ryland's cylinder black is the best paint, as it is resistant to oil and petrol. Aluminium paint is not a substitute for cleaning and polishing and should never be used anywhere except on the exhaust system. It will not be necessary even on these parts if they have been metallised but if you wish to avoid the expense of this type of finish something else will have to be done or your nice clean engine will be marred by a rusty manifold. Ordinary aluminium paint is no use as it soon burns off, but we have found that "Protective Coating AL/50" made by Metallic Coatings Limited is very good. This material is a type of paint, and applied with a brush it gives a very nice aluminium finish which is extremely durable and rustproof. It must be used only on the exhaust system as it needs to be baked and this is the only position where it is likely to receive this treatment.

The wheels will of course have been washed with the body but the effect will be completely ruined if the tires have been left in a muddy state, so these also should have been well washed. They may now be given a smart appearance by a dressing with tyre paint but an even better finish will be produced by polishing with black boot polish which is also the best finish for rubber pedal pads and rubber covered running boards. If your car is an open model make sure that the hood is neatly furled and covered with a well fitting hood envelope. Check your tool kit and make sure that all the items are in a clean condition and neatly stored away.

Originality

You may have been lucky enough to have found a completely original and almost unused motor-car tucked away in a heated garage, but since this is now becoming a very rare experience, especially with Vintage models, it is much more likely that you will have had to carry out a considerable amount of restoration. Originality marking is somewhat debatable as if you had a 1920 car with original battery, tires, water hoses, sparking plugs and ignition leads it would be very unlikely to be a good runner or even roadworthy and if it was completely original it would not even comply with the law. It is obvious that certain alterations and additions will have to be made—such as two rear lights which are now obligatory—but do try to keep everything as near as possible to the original in style, material and finish. Chromium plating should not be used to replace nickel plating however labour-saving this may be, neither should cellulose finish be used on a car which was turned out new with coach painting. If you have the hood re-covered use a cloth similar to the original, the vynide leather cloth type of material which is used on modern convertibles is not the correct wear for a Vintage car on any occasion. Do not fit accessories which are obviously modern in design but try to find Vintage pieces if you need any replacements. You should even be careful if you are repainting the car to use a colour which is in keeping with the period of the car. Many Vintage cars now have coloured wings, the fact having been forgotten that in the early Vintage period most of the cheaper cars had black stove-enamelled mudguards.

Before you start for the meeting make sure that you have in the car the following cleaning materials. A wet sponge and leather in polythene bags, plenty of clean dry dusters, a brush for the carpets and a brush for the boot polish, tins of metal polish and body polish. It is also a good idea to have a piece of cloth or ribbed rubber to cover the carpets so that they arrive in a clean condition even if your passengers have walked in hot tar or gear oil. When you are showing the car do not leave it strewn with luggage or articles of clothing, these should all be removed, and remember to turn off the petrol when you stop the engine to prevent any chance of flooding.

You may be required to stay with the car to start the engine or to answer questions but if you are not, do not leave the car with the bonnet locked, also do not chatter with or get in the way of the judges as they will probably have a lot of work to do in a very short time and spectators are troublesome enough in this respect.

You will doubtless by now have arrived at the conclusion that this *concours* business is a frightful lot of hard work but we are sure that a win will make you think that it is all well worth while and that you have really enjoyed it. You will also be amazed at how much better your own car looks when it has had expended upon it all the extra work which you would probably never have done without the keen spur of competition.

CHAPTER XIV

THE GARAGE AND WORKSHOP

IF you are determined to keep your Vintage or Thoroughbred car in good condition, and we certainly hope that this is your intention, then it is absolutely necessary to have some form of garage so that the vehicle will at least have protection from the weather. If the car is not stored under cover you will have a continuous battle with the elements and this will eventually result in your defeat.

You may be lucky and have a house with plenty of outbuildings which can be converted to garages and a workshop, a most interesting and enjoyable job almost as good as rebuilding a car, but if you are not so fortunate you will have to build in either stone, bricks or timber or you can buy one of the prefabricated variety. You may, of course, build the perfect edifice as illustrated in our first book; this will depend on the cash available but the minimum requirements should be quite inexpensive. Architects or builders will not read this chapter but for those others we will give suggestions for the different types of buildings and layout, so that the labour of planning may be eased and some of the worst pitfalls avoided.

Having decided on the type of building you would like, that is apart from alterations to an existing building but not an increase in size, you must start by submitting the plans to your local authority. Failure to carry out this procedure might result in your being forced to remove the building. You may think that you are quite capable of producing your own plans but we can say, most definitely, that it will pay you to have the plans drawn up either by an architect, or in the case of a prefabricated building the plans may be supplied by the manufacturers. An architect's or manufacturer's design will be far more easily submitted and will be much more likely to be passed by your local authority than an amateur's efforts. In any case you should have an interview with the surveyor to the local authority and ascertain if any particular by-laws apply in your area with regard to the foundations, the type of construction and the appearance of the building before you make your choice or submit your plans. He could also give you advice, if you are in doubt, on the suitability of your ground for the type of building that you would like. Once you have had the plans accepted you can either leave it in the hands of the architect who will obtain competitive quotations from several builders or you could do the whole of the constructional work yourself. It might also suit you to do part of the work yourself and have the remainder done by a builder.

For instance, if you have chosen a timber building and you are a good carpenter you might commission a builder to lay the foundations and the floor and you could then carry on with the remainder of the work, or if it is to be a prefabricated building you could do all the erecting.

It is possible that you may not know of a suitable architect and in this case we suggest that you should apply to the president of the local architectural society allied to the Royal Institute of British Architects who will recommend men who will be suitable for your type of work.

Location, Size and Shape

If you are fortunate enough to have a good area of ground available for the new building it is well worth while giving it some thought so that it will be sited in the most suitable position. A mistake at this period will either condemn you to continuous inconvenience or it will necessitate expensive alterations after the building has been finished. If possible have a paved area at least large enough to park the car and furnished with a drain so that the labour of washing down the car can be carried out in some comfort. This space is also very convenient during fine weather for other jobs. Working in the open is far more pleasurable, it is almost essential for inspection, cleaning and polishing due to the better lighting and it is an absolute necessity for spray painting since you are unlikely to have a large enough space indoors equipped with extractor fans. It is not always necessary to have this paved yard in front of the garage. If it can be arranged a better position is behind the building for greater privacy and, if access cannot be obtained at the side of the garage, additional doors could be fitted in the back of the building and you could then drive right through. Try to position the doors to give ease of access as you may acquire a large car with a poor lock and, should you be having a garage for more than one car, if possible have it wide enough to place the cars side by side with the workshop behind rather than the cars one behind the other with the workshop space at the side. It is such a nuisance to have to put that wheel on again with the job half finished so that you can get out the other car to go down to the local when you are thirsty. An even better arrangement for those who possess more than one car is to have separate garages. The largest of these buildings will be the working garage and since most cars are from five to six feet wide, then a width of ten feet from wall to wall will give about two feet each side; this is the minimum for working on a car. We have both worked in the past in narrower buildings but it is extremely inconvenient and the car is constantly in need of being moved from one side of the garage to the other. If you are unable to do this, for instance when the car is reposing on jack stands with the wheels removed, then every time that you bend down your backside collides with the wall and the resultant impetus given to your anatomy causes your front teeth to be knocked out on some part of the body, so do try to get a working garage with a minimum width of ten feet. The length will depend on the car on which you will be working and this certainly does vary to rather a large extent but, since you may change your car and the length may grow and the garage is unlikely to do so, then it is better to aim for the longest space possible. The other garage or garages will only be required for storage, they can therefore be of such a size as just to accommodate the car with ease, that is, there must be sufficient space at least to open the door of a saloon as it is very tiring to be forced to spend the night in the car if you are unable to get out. The great advantage of this arrangment of separate garages is that you are not taking into the working garage a car which is possibly wet or, even worse, covered with snow so that the floor is flooded with water, the resultant moisture in the atmosphere causing rusting of tools, machines and the car on which work is proceeding. The workshop, or machine shop may be part of this working garage or it may be an adjoining building.

Other points to be considered are the distance that you will have to bring the water and electricity supply, as a long run underground for the latter can be quite expensive. The proximity of neighbours who may be disturbed by the noise when you are having a bout of engine tuning also warrants consideration. If possible arrange the site and also the design of the buildings so that should you require more space then enlargement is readily carried out, as whatever you may think in the initial stages, Vintage addicts have a habit of gradually adding to their fleet of vehicles and also in most cases to their stock of spares. In any case build the longest garage and workshop that you can afford and that can be fitted into the space available, and unless you are a millionaire it will probably be better for you and the furtherance of your hobby to have a garage and workshop large enough for comfortable working but of the cheaper variety. So long as it is sufficiently durable this will be better than a super quality erection which is so small that it is only possible to work on the car in an upright position.

If you are able to have a garage and workshop of brick or stone construction you will no doubt employ an architect and have the building designed to blend with your house. You should, however, study his plans very carefully to make quite sure that you will be getting the most convenient internal lay-out. He may be the most competent man in his profession but even so it is unlikely that he will know anything about your hobby. It is you, therefore, who must advise him as to the details that you will require.

Windows

The position of the windows is very important and the more that you have the less likely that you will need to use artificial light during the daytime, this you will find is not only much more agreeable but it is also

X *The outbuildings of Richard Wheatley's house as purchased*

XI *The same outer shell converted into a two-car garage and workshop by the owner. The main entrance is in the end remote from the camera*

XII *A part of the garage portion of Brian Morgan's motor house. The whole of this building was erected by the owner*

XIII *The workshop portion of the motor house showing lathe, drilling and milling machines*

less tiring to the eyes and after all you will be working for pleasure. Decide on the position of your bench and any machines you may be thinking of installing and have windows in the best position to give good lighting to these points. Small windows in a high position are no use to work by. Don't forget that right of light is not yours to take, if your building is on a neighbour's boundary and you place windows so that they can overlook his land then he could block them up in the first few years if he should be so inclined, so it would be necessary in this case to get the matter settled in a proper manner before the design was finally approved. If possible have top lighting in that part of the garage where you propose to work on the car; this can be either wired glass or one of the new corrugated transparent plastic materials. Daylight over the car is a great benefit particularly when there is any indoor painting to be done.

Type of Door

There is no doubt that the up-and-over type of door is by far the best since this pattern takes up a great deal less space and also it is not affected by a high wind when it is in the open position. It also has the great advantage that the runners and all the mechanism for this type of door are situated inside the building and are therefore not exposed to the weather, so that they can be kept clean and well lubricated thus ensuring permanent ease of operation. However, if you are fitting an up-and-over door make a careful check of the measurements during the opening process if the garage is to be a tight fit on the car, particularly if your car is of the high, square-backed and closed variety. If your car should be an open tourer then you must check the measurements with the hood in the raised position as it is most disconcerting to arrive home on some dark and wet night only to find that when you try to close the garage door it jams on the back hood stick. The vertical jointed type of door running in a curved floor track is deadly as not only does it reduce some of the available garage width but it prevents you putting any shelves or fittings on the wall at the side where it is parked when in the open position. Even worse than this the track fills with water and dirt and then starts to rust away so that the door which you at first thought operated so easily soon jams and eventually jumps out of its track altogether. The traditional hinge pattern of door is, of course, perfectly satisfactory so long as it is well made and supported on adequate hinges, but this type must be fitted with some form of stop to prevent it being slammed against the car in a high wind. The stop should be of a strong construction and preferably fixed on the top edge of the door.

Roofs

There are quite a number of different materials for roof covering and in choosing one of these the aim is to select a type which is not only weatherproof and durable but also one which is a poor conductor, so that you preserve a more equable temperature in the interior of the building. The best materials are either slates, tiles or stone-slates but even these coverings will be much improved if they are lined with roofing felt, particularly if for any reason you are unable to employ a steep enough pitch. This should be from 22° to 33° for slates, depending on the size of the slates, and 45° for tiles. The cheaper type of covering is corrugated asbestos, this makes a good weatherproof roof which is very durable but it should be lined for insulation if you wish to preserve the warmth in winter and to keep out the heat in summer. This type of covering, if it is unlined, is very subject to condensation due to its high degree of conductivity and if, therefore, you do not propose to have any form of lining you must at least treat the inside of the sheets with silicone lacquer to prevent the formation of alkaline drips which would ruin your paintwork. A better form of roof which is also not too expensive is one made from 2 in. strawboard covered with two layers of roofing felt, this type of roof will give excellent insulation and it should wear well but care must be taken to see that the felt is kept in good order and is not punctured. Roofing felt can be dressed with bitumen but not with coal-tar. There are, of course, other forms of roof but in a book of this type it is only possible to mention the more commonly used ones. Flat roofs are not to be recommended due to the difficulty of making them waterproof without being very expensive and we do not approve of corrugated iron for any part of the building as this material deteriorates very rapidly and is generally unsightly.

Rainwater

It should not be forgotten that a large roof will collect a lot of water during wet weather, this is not any problem for the average sized garage if it is surrounded by soft ground such as flower beds or a shrubbery, in any other case gutters will have to be provided and the water must be led into some form of drain or soak-away. A drain is the method to be recommended if it is at all possible as soak-aways gradually become silted up especially if they are used to accommodate the effluent from a car wash. When designing the guttering it is as well to remember that both guttering and down-pipes are now made in aluminium and plastic, both these materials are much less liable to corrosion and fracture than the iron variety that we have formerly had to contend with.

Floors

These days floors are basically concrete on top oι ιne earth, but the floor should be laid really flat as you may require to use it as a datum point for the taking of measurements such as setting up the springs of the car. The minimum thickness is 4 in. and the surface should be treated with a hardener as untreated concrete is a most prolific source of dust. An even better floor would be 4 in. of concrete with a top dressing of 1½ in. of granolithic, again treated with a hardener such as Lithurin. A great luxury would be a concrete floor covered with either wood blocks or quarry tiles. Wood block flooring is very kind to the feet but it is more suitable for the work shop as if it were used in the garage troubles would undoubtedly be experienced with it due to the swelling of the wood if a wet car was run on to it. Quarry tiles are not so pleasant for walking on as wood but this type of floor does not suffer from the wet, it is very easy to clean and it is, of course, dustless like the Spyker.

Prefabricated Garages

The main types of construction for prefabricated garages are, in order of merit, concrete, timber and metal.

The concrete type is the most durable but unfortunately it has bad insulating properties and in consequence is very subject to condensation and it should therefore be lined, this will be additional to the normal specification. Concrete has the great advantage that it is fireproof but any fittings or shelves are difficult to attach to the structure. However, some makers do provide special arrangements for this.

The timber building is not so durable as the concrete construction and it is also dangerous from the fire risk point of view and for this reason it may be subject to by-laws. Some authorities will not allow garages of timber construction to be built near to houses. The great advantages are that this type is the least likely to suffer from condensation, it is very easily modified if necessary and shelving or fittings are very simple to fix. It is absolutely necessary for the timber to have some form of treatment against decay and certain manufacturers use pre-treated wood, this is far better than treatment after assembly which only protects the surface. Timber garages should be built on a brick or concrete foundation making sure that the lower part of the woodwork is well above the ground level as damp will soon cause rotting of the wood.

Metal garages, although inexpensive and of course, completely fireproof, are the least durable. They are very subject to temperature variation, are noisy and in constant need of painting unless they are clad in galvanised sheets but in this case the appearance is very poor. They soon start to look shabby and in our opinion they are generally undesirable.

The following is a list of prefabricated garages, together with the type of construction and the firm who manufactures them.

Make	*Maker's Name*	*Construction*
BANBURY	Banbury Buildings Ltd.	Pre-cast concrete
BATLEY	Ernest Batley Ltd.	Pre-cast concrete
BELCON	Bell & Webster Ltd.	Pre-cast concrete
BISON	Bison (Garages) Ltd.	Pre-cast concrete
COMPTON	Sectional Concrete Buildings Ltd.	Pre-cast concrete
MARLEY	Marley Concrete Ltd.	Pre-cast concrete
PRATTEN	F. Pratten & Co. Ltd.	Timber: wood frame covered with asbestos sheeting; steel frame covered with corrugated asbestos; steel frame covered with galvanised sheeting
SUTCLIFFE	F. H. Sutcliffe Ltd.	Timber: timber and asbestos; pre-cast concrete. This manufacturer uses pre-treated timber

We feel that out of the above list Banbury Buildings Ltd. seem to give the best range of models. In any case get the up-to-date literature and the full particulars before you make your choice. Most manufacturers will supply a drawing of the building for you to submit to your local authority; if this is not available we suggest that you go to another manufacturer. Most manufacturers do not supply the foundations and none of them supply the floors so that you will either have to do this job yourself or you can employ a builder. In the case of normal concrete garages the manufacturers will always supply particulars of the foundation and the floor that will be required. Bison (Garages) Limited can supply ground beams which will form the foundation by merely laying them on levelled ground, the floor is then put in afterwards.

Electricity Supply

Unless this happens to be your line of business you should get the advice of a qualified contractor before laying any mains underground and even the interior wiring must be done to the Institute of Electrical Engineers' specification.

Water Supply

It is probably better to have this work done by a qualified plumber but in any case make sure that all water mains underground are sufficiently deep to be protected from the frost, the minimum depth is 3 ft. Any connections to the supply must be made by arrangement with the Water Supply Authority.

Heating

Apart from the fact that working in an unheated garage or workshop during the winter is not very pleasant, lack of warmth will promote condensation, and therefore rusting and corrosion of steel and aluminium parts. Even a small amount of continuous heat will prevent this trouble. Electric heating is quite the most easily installed and this type of heating has the great advantage that it requires no maintenance. You could use either tubular heaters or Dimplex oil-filled radiators with thermostatic control. An alternative form of heating is by hot water pipes and radiators supplied by a boiler which can be either fired by gas, oil or solid fuel, the latter is the most inexpensive to run but a fair amount of maintenance is required. The boiler should be installed outside the garage due to the risk of fire. A fairly cheap type of system would be pipes and a boiler as is used for greenhouses and this you could install yourself. You might even be able to pick up some second-hand piping as this is the most expensive part of the system.

Lighting and Power

Good lighting is essential and you should have a bracket lamp for the vice and for each machine. Anglepoise lamps are very good indeed but there are other types that are quite satisfactory and much cheaper. Overhead lighting can be of the fluorescent type, this form of lighting is cheaper to run and throws less shadows than the tungsten lamp. Inspection lamps should be of low voltage for safety, they can be 12 volt run from a mains transformer. A shock from faulty insulation can be dangerous at mains voltage when standing on a concrete floor and particularly if you are working in a damp pit. Very fine lighting in a pit can be achieved by bulkhead lamps fixed on the sides, these should be ironclad and the wiring must be in conduit. All the wiring for the garage is better if it is laid in conduits. Make sure that you have enough 3-pin sockets for your power tools and trickle charger to avoid having the place festooned with long leads.

Water and Gas

If you have the water laid on a great luxury is to have a basin fitted in the garage for the washing of hands, leathers and sponges but you will, of course, require to have the waste led away to a drain. There is no need to have a gas supply from the mains as calor gas is so very good and in any case, for a blow pipe, town gas will require a supply of compressed air but calor gas does not. You will have to get the special blow pipe for use with calor gas.

Benches and Shelves

The main bench should be of rigid construction and must be bolted to the floor, metal legs cross-braced are very good. Make sure that you have an adequate amount of shelving and storage space so that you can keep everything off the floor, it is worth going to a lot of trouble to achieve ease of sweeping. Long narrow shelves about 3 ft. high and fixed to the walls each side of the car are very useful for tools and parts when you are working on the car. Try to keep all spares, fittings and materials in drawers or cabinets. There are some very good metal chests of drawers available ex-W.D. at quite low prices, these chests are also very good for storing those tools that are not used continuously.

The Pit

Unless you are wealthy enough to have an electric hoist then a pit is almost a necessity. It is very exhausting and somewhat difficult to clean underneath a car if you do not have a pit and some jobs are quite impossible. When building the pit try to make it about 3 ft. longer than the largest car that you are likely to work on. If you cannot have a pit and also provided you have sufficient head room, a useful system to ease the work on long jobs is to have wooden stands made in the form of boxes with open bottoms. The car is then jacked up and the stands are placed in position one at a time working at alternative ends of the chassis until the desired height has been achieved (see fig. 20). When not in use these stands make very good and strong movable benches. Never work under a car which has been jacked up and the wheels removed unless it has been placed on rigid jack stands as this is a very dangerous practice—people have been killed in this way through the jack slipping.

Lifting Tackle

If the building is of brick construction then an R.S.J. can be put in to take the chain block for lifting heavy parts. This joist should be above the centre and parallel with the car. If the building is not suitable for installing an R.S.J. and you have any heavy lifting to do you will have to make up a set of shear-legs on which to hang the chain block. These sheer-legs can be made from galvanised water pipe (see fig. 21).

General Garage Tools

We have dealt with hand tools in our previous book but there are a

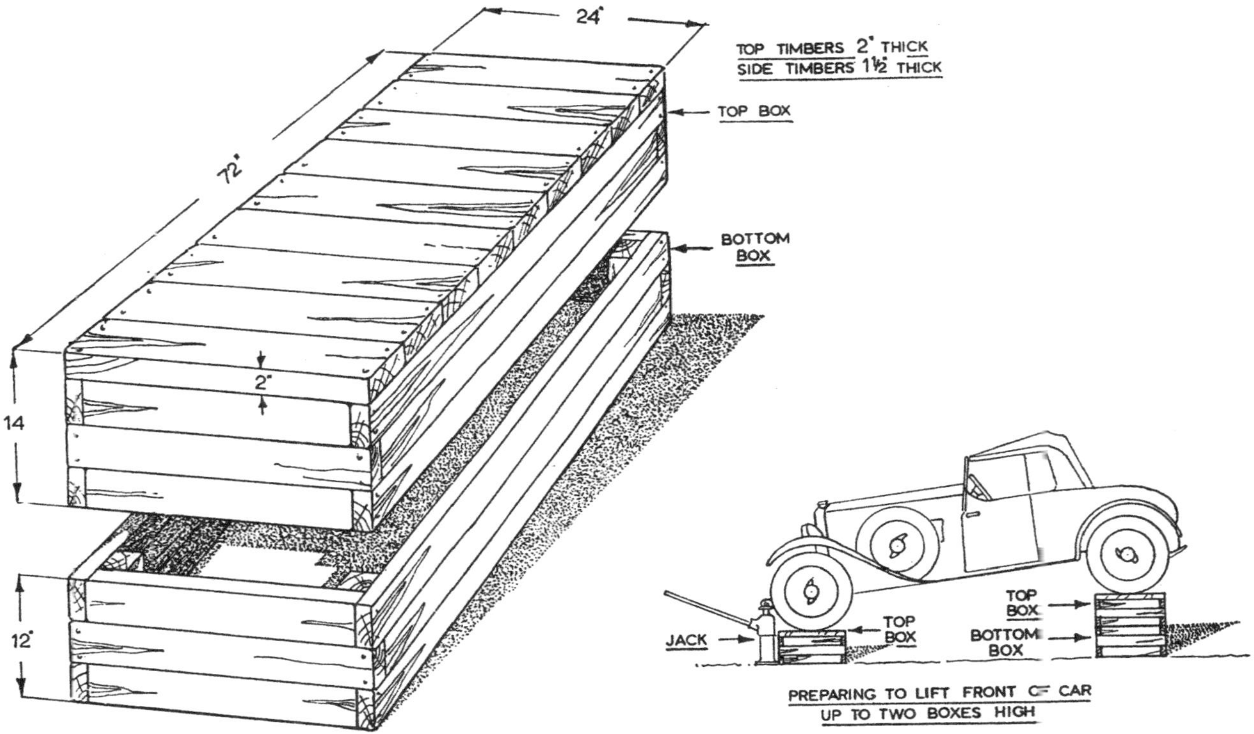

20 *Jacking boxes*

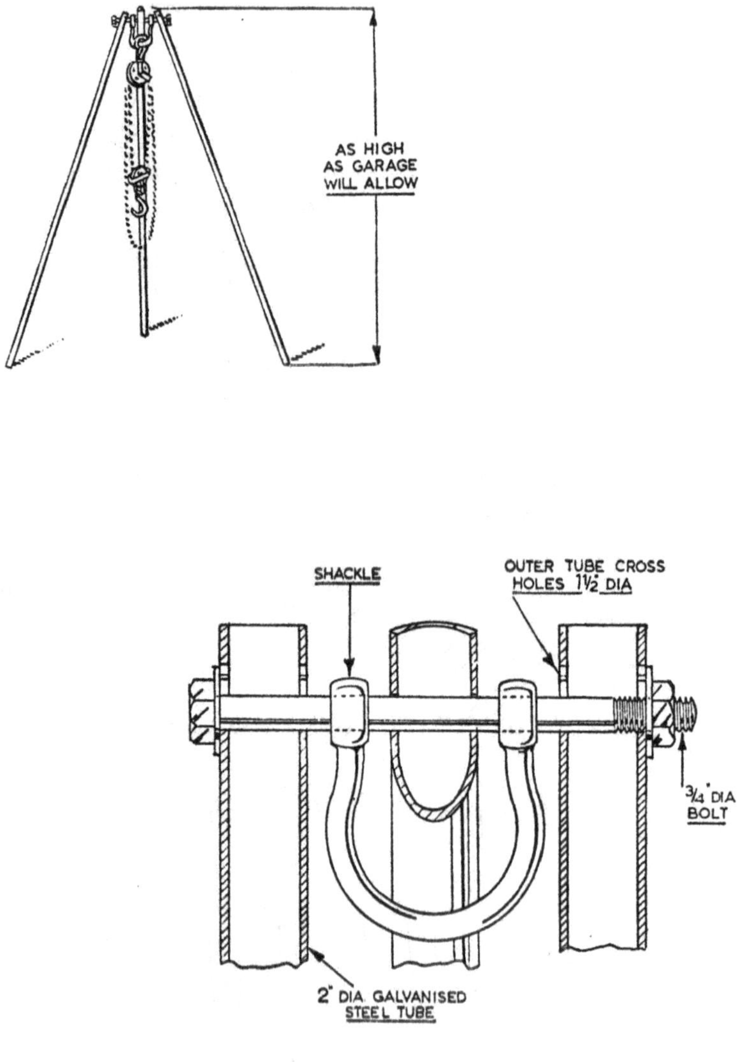

21 *Sheer-legs*

certain number of tools and pieces of equipment that are required for use in the garage itself.

You will require at least two jacks, these can be either screw, quick-lift or hydraulic, even better would be to have one jack and four strong jack stands. The quick-lift type of jack on wheels and with a long handle is very useful but its use is marred by the liability to fall over the handle.

An air compressor for tire inflation and spray painting is useful. If you have a supply of compressed air you can have a paraffin spray for cleaning down all oily mechanical parts.

To complete the efficiency of your garage the following equipment should be included:

Greasing and oiling equipment.
A wheel-brace, wheel spanner or copper hammer depending on the type of your wheels.
A receptacle for draining engines and gearboxes.
A large tin and brushes for cleaning parts with paraffin.
A dust sheet large enough to cover each car completely.
Sponges, leather and wheel brush.

CHAPTER XV

THE CHOICE AND USE OF SIMPLE MACHINE TOOLS

WHILE we realise that only a minority of our readers will have machine tools at their disposal at present, we do feel that as the years pass it will become increasingly necessary to own at least a lathe and a drilling machine to make the replacement parts needed to keep your car on the road. Obviously those who can afford to have the parts made by a firm of machinists have no worries in this respect, but this practice becomes more expensive every year and as the price of one-off jobs rises so does it become more and more of a proposition to buy the necessary plant to do it yourself. The other aspect of this problem, and equally important in our view, is the sheer convenience of being able to make a piece the same day as you decide that you want it instead of waiting in a queue for somebody else to make it for you. Another attraction of being self sufficient in this respect is the great satisfaction of making a spare part, probably as good if not better than the original, without having to rely on others to help you. This satisfaction has to be experienced to be fully understood but we can assure you that it is very real and gives one great contentment.

In this chapter we propose to go through the process of making some typical commonly needed parts, describing each operation in sequence as we should make them. We do not propose to describe the basic arts of turning, milling and drilling which are very adequately dealt with already in a score of technical manuals. We shall, however, mention any out of the ordinary small tools which we have found to be particularly useful.

Before describing the processes we had better mention the various machine tools which are necessary. First the lathe, by far the most universally useful machine it is possible to own. We would recommend one with a centre height of between 6 in. and 7 in. and preferably with a detachable gap bed as ideal for this sort of work. Screw cutting is essential but the age of the machine is quite immaterial providing it is in good condition. Old-fashioned belt driven lathes can often be picked up at a second-hand machinery dealers for very low prices and a second-hand electric motor to drive it can often be bought at the same time. If space is a difficulty try to find one with as short a bed as possible as you will rarely need to make a long job. A second-hand lathe is often without a range of chucks or the chuck that has been left on when the lathe was sold will probably be worn out. It is better to pay less for an older lathe and to buy some new chucks and tool holders, which will last for a life time if properly looked after, than to spend to the limit on the actual lathe.

The ideal set of equipment to go with a lathe for our type of work is as follows:

1 3-in. 3-jaw chuck with normal and reversed jaws.
1 7-in. 3-jaw chuck with normal and reversed jaws.
1 4-in. 4-jaw chuck.
1 9-in. 4-jaw chuck.
1 10-in. face plate
1 ½-in. drill chuck for the tailstock.
1 Fixed steady.
1 Travelling steady.
1 Collet chuck with collets ⅛–1 in. in $\frac{1}{16}$ in. steps.
1 Toolbit holder to take $\frac{5}{16}$ in.-square H.S. bits. Straight.
1 Toolbit holder to take $\frac{5}{16}$ in.-square H.S. bits. Left crank.
1 Toolbit holder to take $\frac{5}{16}$ in.-square H.S. bits. Right crank.
1 Parting tool blade holder to take ¾ in. blade.
1 Running back centre.
1 Fixed back centre.
1 Boring tool holder to take ½-in. diameter bars, complete with various lengths of boring bar.

With this equipment practically any job can be tackled and there is, of course, no need to get it all at once. An essential adjunct to the lathe is a bench grinder which must be power driven. It is no good thinking that you can grind a lathe tool properly while cranking a hand driven grinder; it is just not possible. A 6-in. diameter wheel of medium grit running at 3,000 r.p.m. is necessary and if you do not want the expense of buying the ready made article a wheel can be mounted on the end of an electric motor of ¼ h.p. or more. The wheel must be guarded round as much of its periphery as possible as well as both sides. If you buy a normal double ended bench grinder you can take off the wheel and guard at one end and mount a 6-in. rotary wire mop in its place which you will find very useful for cleaning up old parts.

The drilling machine best suited to our work is a ½-in. capacity pillar machine mounted on the floor with a table that will swing out of the way to make room for drilling long jobs. A speed range of 300–2,500 r.p.m. is adequate. If this is out of the question you can consider a ½-in. capacity electric brace with a bench mounting attachment. This will only have two speeds at the most which is a disadvantage, but it is very much better than not having a drilling machine and you can use the brace separately for jobs on the actual car itself. A drilling vice, preferably with jaws that incorporate Vees for holding round stock, will be very useful as will a pair of large V-blocks, say 3 in., to support any shaft which you may wish to cross-drill. Naturally a drilling machine is no good without high speed twist drills of which you can never have enough. To build up a collection we would recommend starting with a set of fractional size drills $\frac{1}{16}$–$\frac{1}{2}$ in. in $\frac{1}{16}$ in. steps followed by a complete set of number sizes (1–60) and then a set of letter sizes (A–Z). Larger diameters than $\frac{1}{2}$ in. start to become very expensive and are better bought one at a time as they are needed. Ifyour drilling machine has a taper bored spindle then buy drills larger than $\frac{1}{2}$ in. with taper shanks to fit this. Turning down the shanks of large drills to suit a $\frac{1}{2}$-in. chuck is not a very good practice although one is often forced to do it when such a drill has to be used in an electric brace.

We have now covered the two most essential machine tools but if you want to go one further you will have to make the choice between a vertical milling machine and a metal cutting band saw. In our experience you will use the saw more often than the miller and it is a great time and labour saver. However, there are many instances where you could do the job just as well with hand tools by the expenditure of a great deal more sweat. There are certain jobs which cannot be done without a vertical milling machine although in some cases the lathe can take its place, again taking more time as it is not the ideal tool. Having had both for a number of years it is difficult to say which one would rather do without, but perhaps on balance the band saw is the greater luxury.

A convenient size of vertical miller has a table of 14 in. × 9 in. and a spindle with collets $\frac{1}{8}$–$\frac{1}{2}$ in. in $\frac{1}{16}$ steps. Workpiece clamps can be made in the workshop but a good milling vice is essential. If you can run to a vice which can be tilted to any desired angle so much the better, but many normal jobs can be tackled with a plain parallel jaw vice. The ultimate luxury is a rotating table fitted with a detachable 3-jaw 6-in. chuck with which polygons can be milled and also rings of holes can be bored accurately on a given pitch circle. As with the lathe it is often possible to pick up a vertical miller of an outdated design for an absurdly low price probably only discarded because it had no built-in motor drive. Such a machine is bound to need some overhaul but as you already feel able to work on the complicated mechanism of your motor car you should not be detered by the relative simplicity of a milling machine. A useful set of milling cutters to start with would be $\frac{1}{16}$–$\frac{1}{2}$ in. diameter in steps of $\frac{1}{16}$ in.

Finally the band saw. Like all other tools, once you have had one you cannot understand how you ever managed without it. It can be used to cut wood, plastic or metal, providing it has a correct range of speeds and the thickness of the material which it will cut is only limited by the size of the machine. When choosing a band saw remember first to check on its speed range—one that will not go slow enough to cut steel is useless for your type of work—and secondly, remember that the wider the throat between the two sides of the saw the less will you be restricted when cutting out of sheet material. There are sawing machines now available with three wheels instead of the more conventional two and this design gives a very wide throat which is very convenient. A tilting table is also a great advantage for cutting at an angle. If a band saw is out of the question an alternative is the electric hand saw which is like a key hole saw only driven electrically. There are several makes of these now on the market but again make sure that the one you choose has available a blade for cutting steel. All makes of this type reciprocate rather fast for steel cutting, being primarily designed for use on wood and plastic, but certain makers will supply a blade for steel and with constant application of cutting oil to the blade they work quite well. The one advantage of an electric hand saw is that you can take it to the job and can cut out holes in flat or even curved surfaces.

Examples of Machining

1. *Shackle Pin and Bush*

Before starting on the pin you will have to decide whether you will be able to get it case hardened when it is finished. If so it should be made from a good quality low carbon steel such as Flather's UBAS, if it is not going to be hardened then a piece of harder-wearing steel should be used such as Kayser Elison's KE.805 in the 60-ton U.T.S. condition. As you will probably be making more than one pin and bush it is as well to make a plan of action which will allow you to do all of one operation on every pin before starting on the next operation. This principle applies to all jobs where more than one of anything is being made and saves a considerable amount of time in tool setting.

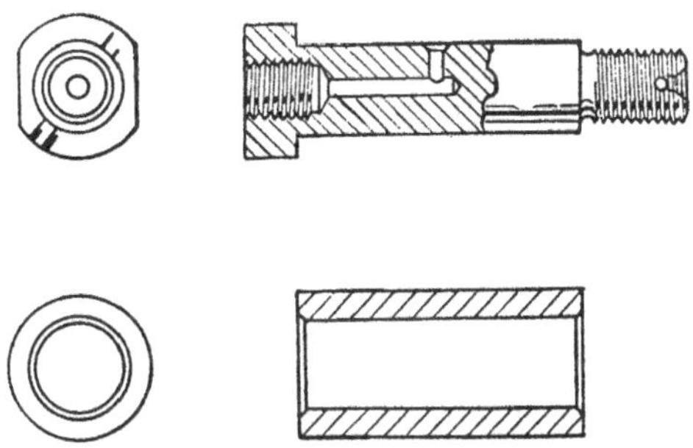

22 *Shackle pin and bush*

Start by facing the end of the bar and centre drilling the end. Then draw sufficient bar out of the chuck to allow machining one complete pin and engage the running centre. Using a side cutting tool with sufficient radius ground on it not to produce a dead sharp corner under the head of the pin, turn the three diameters of head, shank and screwed portion. Then part off, leaving an allowance for facing the head and repeat the process on however many pins you have to make. The next operation will be to undercut the threaded end to allow a run out for the screw-cutting tool. Hold the head relatively lightly in the chuck and engage the centre, then tighten the chuck. A round-nosed tool ground to the correct form will now produce a radiused undercut the depth of which should be just below the core diameter of the thread. Repeat this on all the pins and then set up for screw cutting whatever pitch of thread is required. As each pin is put in the lathe use the screw-cutting tool to form the chamfer on the end of the pin before using it to cut the thread. By noting the readings on the cross slide dial you can produce an identical chamfer on each pin and also, after making the first thread carefully to size, you can repeat the same very quickly on all the remainder. Having cut the thread nearly down to size it can be finished with a button die which will put the requisite rounded crest on the thread which cannot be made with a single point screw cutting tool. Do not be tempted to put the whole thread on with a die as if this is in the normal die-stock the thread will not be true.

The next operation will be to hold the shank in the chuck and to face the head to length. Again by doing this one operation on all the pins at one setting of the tool a lot of time is saved. At the same time the oil hole can be drilled and the larger diameter grease nipple tapping size hole put in. The final operation in the lathe will be to chamfer the head.

There are two cross-drillings needed, one for the oil hole and one for the split pin. You will make a far better job of these if you make a very simple drilling jig for each of them, as drilling vertically into a rounded surface is not easy with an unsupported drill. All you need to do is to drill a hole up the length of a piece of square or hexagon bar the same diameter as the shank of the pin. Drill a cross-hole in the right position in the hexagon bar and as you will be drilling on one of the flats of the jig this is very simple. Then slip each pin into the jig and drill the oil cross-hole. The jig for the split pin hole can be made from a hexagon bar tapped to the right size and cross-drilled so that when each pin is screwed into it up to the shoulder at the end of the thread the split pin hole will come in the correct position.

Finally the two flats have to be milled on. If you have a vertical milling machine and rotary table the method will be obvious. If you have not then use the lathe. An end mill can be put in the chuck and each pin can be held in the tool post, preferably in a Vee block such as is used for holding a boring bar. Mill off the required depth of one flat and then turn the pin in the Vee-block using the one flat as a guide together with a square standing on the slideway of the cross slide to set the pin exactly right to get the second flat parallel to the first one.

If the pin is to be case-hardened the very best practice is to leave a grinding allowance on the shank but as you will be unlikely to have grinding facilities make the pin the correct size and polish it with fine emery cloth after hardening. The bushes can be made to suit any discrepancies in diameter afterwards. The thread should be copper plated before hardening so that this portion is left in the soft state.

The bushes will be made from chill cast phosphor bronze bar. Here again split the job down into separate operations. Rough turn the outside diameter to 0·010 in. above the finished size. Drill the centre hole $\frac{1}{16}$ in. under the finished diameter and part the bush off the bar slightly over the necessary length. Then hold each bush in the chuck and bore the inside to the finished dimension with a single point boring tool. If the bush is to be a press fit into the spring eye make the bore 0·002 in. oversize to allow for the bush compressing on assembly. Face the ends to length and chamfer the bore at each end. Finally put each bush onto an expanding mandrel and finish the outside diameter. The bush will now be concentric which it will not be if made in any other way and, although this is not very important in the case of a shackle bush, it can be vital in other instances such as a little-end bush. The expanding mandrel is very easily made by turning a piece of steel or brass down to about 0·005 in. above the diameter required and drilling a suitable hole down the centre to take a taper pin. If you have a taper drill so much the better but a parallel hole will do quite well. The rod is then taken out of the lathe and two saw slots cut part way down its length across its diameter and at right angles to each other. It is then put back in the lathe and skimmed to the correct size and it must be left in the chuck until all the bushes are finished. Once removed it will never run true again. The bush is then put onto the mandrel and the taper pin tapped up the centre hole which will expand the mandrel very tightly into the bush. A screw thread put on the large end of the taper pin allows a nut to be used as the extractor for the pin (see fig. 23).

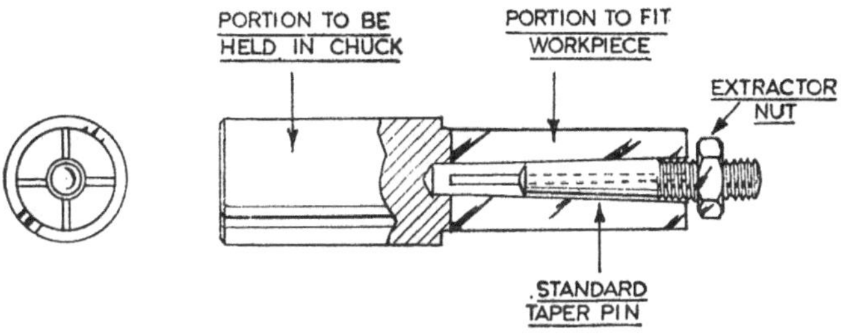

23 *Expanding mandrel*

2. *Brake Drums*

Very many cars thirty years and more of age are now badly in need of a new set of brake drums. Although we cannot pretend that making a new set is an easy task, it is possible providing that you can find a foundry willing to make the castings in a suitable quality of iron. Spheroidal Graphite Iron or S.G.I. is very suitable for this purpose and being as strong as the mild steel from which your original drums were probably made the same dimensions will still suffice. An improvement can be made by thickening up the flange of the drum in a ribbed form which will no doubt make your braking better than the original. You can either make your own wood pattern, building it up from pieces glued together and finishing by turning, or possibly you can call upon the services of a professional pattern maker. In either case do not attempt to cast the ribs but leave the flange thick enough to turn the ribs in after casting. Leave ⅛ in. of machining on all surfaces, inside and out as the drum must be machined all over to achieve a reasonable state of balance.

Having obtained the castings proceed to machine them but bear in mind it is essential that the drum will run true when mounted on its hub which means that the locating bore which fits onto the hub spigot must be absolutely true with the working bore of the drum. That this will be so means that a dummy hub must be machined and left in the chuck while each drum in turn is mounted on it and the bore finally machined. No chuck in any lathe ever runs dead true and for accurate concentricity some device which has been machined in the lathe and not removed must always be used.

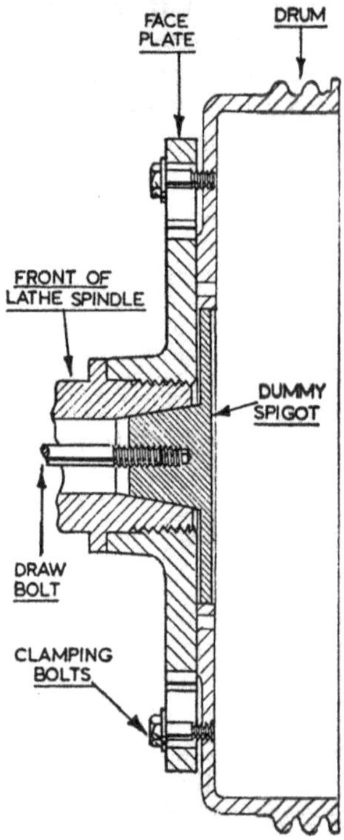

24 *Final operation of machining brake drum*

Start by mounting the drum in a three jaw chuck, expanding the jaws into the rough cast centre hole with the open end of the drum facing the tool post. Get the drum running as true as possible and take a skim off the end of the flange until it has just cleaned up. Repeat this on all the drums and then mark out on a suitable pitch circle, to be clear of the centre boss, three clamping holes which can be drilled and tapped ⅜ in. B.S.F. The drum can then be clamped to the face plate with its open end towards the face plate with three ⅜ in. B.S.F. bolts passing through the face plate and engaging the threads in the clamping holes. Get the drum running as true as possible before finally tightening the bolts. Now machine to finished dimensions all the outside of the drum and the bore of the spigot hole. Repeat on each drum in turn paying particular attention to keeping the centre bores exactly right in diameter to be a tap fit on the hubs. Before taking the drum off the face plate mark the pitch circle on which the fixing bolt holes will be drilled, their actual centres can be marked off with a pair of dividers afterwards.

It is now necessary to provide a spigot running true in the lathe so that each drum can be mounted on it and the working surface of the drum machined. As your lathe will probably have a taper bore in its headstock spindle turn a suitable piece of metal—brass will do being easier to machine—with a shank to fit the taper bore and preferably fitted with a draw bolt to hold it in place in the spindle. Pull this into the spindle with the face plate in position and machine the spigot exactly to the diameter of the spigots on your hubs. Each drum can then be put on the spigot and held onto the face plate with shorter $\frac{3}{8}$ in. B.S.F. bolts as shown in fig. 24 and concentricity of hub and drum is assured when the machining is complete.

The three clamping bolt holes can be blanked off with screwed plugs before the drum is fitted to the car.

3. *Brake Operating Lever and Fork Joint*

When the great wave of purism overtakes the owners of quite a number of Vintage cars and they decide to convert their braking systems back from the present temporary hydraulic lash-up to a decent rod and lever operation they will probably find it very difficult to lay their hands on all the original pieces that they so hastily discarded some years previously. Apart from that these two parts are good examples of what can be made in the amateur workshop and the principles applied will equally apply to many other similar parts.

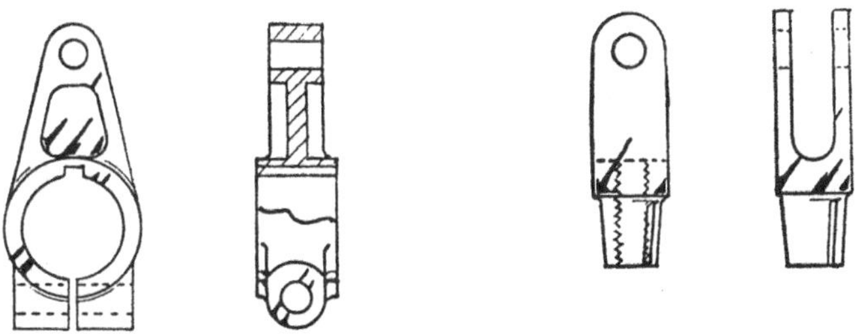

25 *Brake operating lever and fork joint*

Starting with the operating lever, which is typical of those usually found on the end of cross-shafts or brake camshafts, this can best be made from a piece of mild steel plate or bright mild steel bar of the nearest section. First make a drawing of what you are going to make with all the relevant dimensions marked on it. Making a drawing may seem a waste of time if you already have a pattern to work from but it will always save time in the end as, while you are drawing, a plan of action on the various machining operations will form in your head and snags which might have arisen half-way through the job making it impossible to proceed, will be overcome on paper. Rubbing out a mistake on paper is a moment's work; on the job itself there is no eraser.

If you have a number of these levers to make and you don't possess a band saw then it will pay you to make a metal template of the outside shape $\frac{1}{16}$ in. oversize all round and to get someone with the right equipment to flame cut the blanks for you. If you have a band saw or have decided to slog it out with a hack-saw, then mark out the shape on the plate and cut it out leaving sufficient all round for cleaning up. If you are cutting from black mild steel you will have to use material a little thicker than the finished job to clean up both sides.

The next operation is to put in the two holes. Mark out their centres and drill the clevis pin hole in the drilling machine, using a centre drill to start with as a normal twist drill will not pick up a centre punch dot accurately. It will probably be best to drill the hole $\frac{1}{64}$ in. undersize and open it out with the finished size drill which will give a dead size hole. No drill which has been ground free-hand on its point will ever drill exactly the correct diameter from the solid metal owing to eccentricity of the point. If you have a finished size reamer to use so much the better. Next centre-drill the position for the large size hole and clamp the lever onto the face plate of the lathe locating it correctly with the back centre engaged in the centre-drill hole. The large hole can then be drilled and finally bored to size. If you are making more than one lever you will, of course, do each operation on all the levers in turn.

While the job is still in the lathe the key way can be cut. This is achieved by grinding a boring tool bit to act as a key-way slotting tool and mounting it in the tool post. When making the tool use a micrometer to measure it and grind it exactly the right width of the key-way. Set the tool accurately so that the centre line is on the centre height of the lathe spindle and turn the spindle until the lever is in the correct angular position for the key-way to be in the right relationship to the operating end of the lever. The spindle should then be locked which can generally be achieved by engaging the back gears or putting the gearbox into bottom speed in the case of an all-geared headstock. Now, by working the saddle backwards and forwards and gradually feeding on the cut the slotting can be achieved. Use the most robust boring bar which will go through the hole in the lever with the minimum of projection from the tool post to achieve the maximum rigidity in the tool and a really nice key-way will be made.

Remove the lever from the lathe and mark out and drill the pinch-bolt hole and follow this operation by spot-facing the two ends of the lug in which this hole is drilled. This can either be done with a piloted counter-boring tool, a set of which is an exceedingly useful piece of workshop equipment, or with an end mill of the right diameter. In the latter case the workpiece will have to be rigidly clamped, either in the tool post of the lathe or the vice of the vertical miller, as there is a considerable tendency for the end mill to wander when used in this way.

While the lever is still one thickness throughout its length it can be clamped to the table of the vertical miller and the lightening panel milled out on each side. This can be done in the lathe by mounting a shaft of the correct diameter in the tool post and clamping the lever onto it with its own pinch bolt. The milling cutter will, of course, be running in the lathe chuck. Perhaps it would be as well to say that if you are never likely to have a vertical milling machine you should seriously consider either buying or making a milling attachment for your lathe which is interchangeable with the normal tool post but which gives an additional vertical movement to the cross slide. Such an attachment is described in many of the good books available on workshop practice.

A shaft of the right diameter can now be put in the lathe chuck and the lever clamped onto it with its own pinch bolt. There will be no need to put a key into the shaft as the pinch bolt will clamp tightly enough. The end of the centre boss can be skimmed and the lever portion turned down to the right width. Remove the lever and replace it the other way round and repeat the operation on the other side.

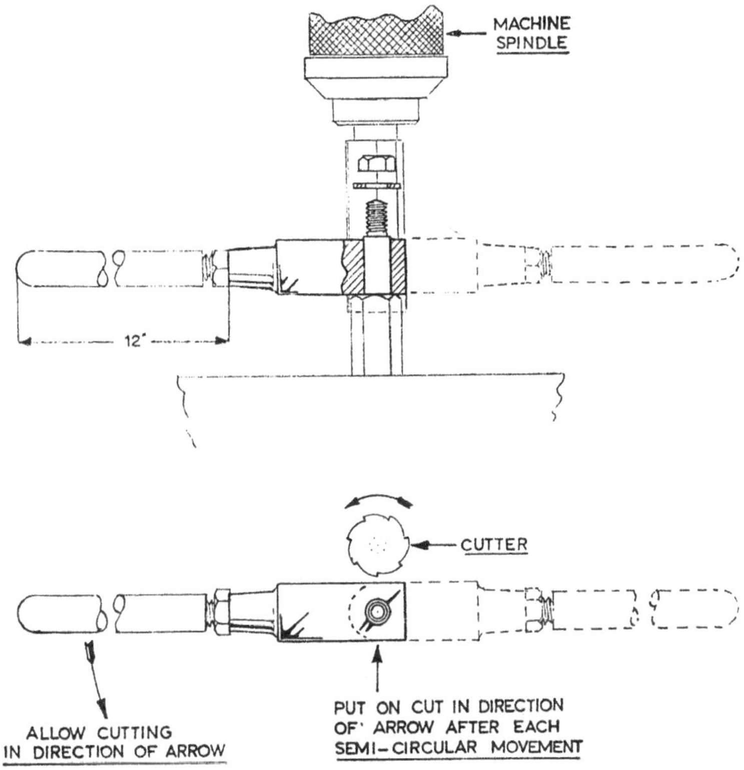

26 *Milling a radius*

The lever is now complete except for filing the outside edge to shape and removing any undesirable sharp corners by hand.

The fork joint is a much more simple job and will be made from square bright-drawn mild steel stock of the right size. Once again if you have more than one to make do each operation on all the pieces separately before going on to the next operation.

Start by putting the whole length of square bar in the four-jaw chuck leaving sufficient protruding for one fork joint plus $\frac{1}{4}$ in. for parting off. Be careful to get the bar running true or the result will look most unprofessional, centre the end and drill and tap the centre hole. Now turn the shank portion which will look better if tapered at about 5° included angle than if it was left parallel. Part the workpiece off the bar and repeat the procedure for as many joints as you are making. Next mark the centre of the clevis pin hole and from this scribe the semi-circular end. Drill in the drilling machine making certain that you keep perfectly at right angles to the axis of the workpiece. Failure to do this will result in either having to enlarge the hole on assembly in order to get the pin through the fork joint and the lever, or you will have to hammer the pin in which will give you sticking brakes. As with the lever use an undersize drill first and the correct size of drill as a reamer for the sake of accuracy.

We now come to rounding off the end in a semi-circle the centre of which coincides with the centre of the clevis pin hole. This can, of course, be filed by hand but there is a method of machining which, although somewhat dicey, is very effective and produces a much more professional job than filing. The principle employed is to mill round the outside with the side of an end mill, the workpiece being mounted on a spindle passing through the clevis pin hole. The maximum rigidity of mounting is needed for this and great care must be taken to avoid a disaster but with the right precautions an excellent job can result. To make the spindle turn a piece of square or hexagon bar down to a diameter which is a nice running fit in the clevis pin hole. Leave 2 in. of hexagon and clamp this vertically in the milling vice. Now thread the fork joint onto this spindle and screw a length of rod into the brake rod hole to act as a handle. The rod should be at least 12 in. long to give good control. Now move the workpiece in towards the cutter and at the same time rotate it on its spindle through a semi-circle until the cutter just touches the most projecting part which will be removed in a true radius. Continue this procedure until the full semi-circle has been cut. We cannot over-emphasise that this needs doing with great care, because if the milling cutter takes control you will have a nasty mess instead of a beautiful job. Always turn the workpiece against the direction of the milling cutter and take off the cut for the reverse semi-circular movement and never get your fingers near the cutter. This principle can be used on many jobs where a radius edge has to be formed concentric to a hole. If you have a rotating table on your milling machine then the job can be properly clamped and rotated without any danger. The operation is illustrated in fig. 26 as applied to a milling machine, but an equally good job can be made in a lathe.

To complete the fork joint the centre slot is milled out by conventional means using a cutter the width of the slot.

4. *Banjo Pipe Connection*

Although it is sometimes possible to buy the correct design of banjo connection there are many non-standard sizes to be found on Vintage cars, especially on certain cooling systems and if one of these becomes corroded away a new one must be made.

To obviate the expense of a casting pattern if only one or two of these are needed, it is quite simple to turn a finished product from a piece of round bar. The most easy machining material for this job is brass which has the added attraction of being non-corrodible in water should your original have been steel or aluminium. Start with a piece of brass rod of a little larger diameter than the spherical end of the banjo and turn the neck portion which should be tapered on its outside to look correct. Drill the pipe hole to the correct depth and the slightly smaller way hole roughly to reach the centre of what will be the spherical portion. Part off the piece leaving enough to make the sphere. Now soft solder a piece of round bar into the pipe hole which can be held in the chuck while the sphere is turned. Make a sheet metal template, if you have no radius gauges, and turn to as near the finished shape as you can. The outside can be given a perfectly spherical form by a means described on page 48 of our previous book but in the case of a banjo some judicious use of a file will probably be good enough.

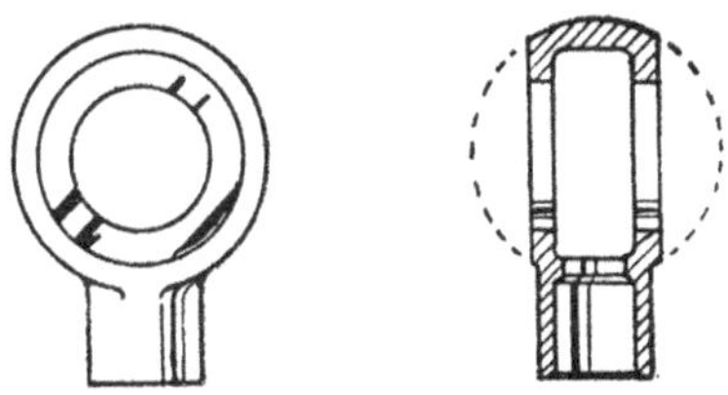

27 *Banjo pipe connection*

Unsolder the rod and holding the sphere in the four jaw chuck face off one side to the correct diameter of flat face and drill the bolt hole. The undercut can also be bored at this stage. As it is very important to have both sealing faces parallel to one another, resist the temptation merely to turn the job round in the chuck when it will be very difficult to set correctly. Turn a mandrel from a piece of rod onto which the bolt hole is a tap fit. A slight taper on the mandrel will achieve a good drive and if the banjo is tapped onto this taper it will be running perfectly true for you to machine the other sealing face.

5. *Spare Wheel Clamping Wing-nut*

The great advance of really good silver solder has somewhat reduced the necessity of using castings for odd shapes such as this example, where three pieces can easily be made and soldered together resulting in a job which has the great virtue of being machined all over with a consequent elimination of all fettling.

This particular piece can be made either in brass or steel, the two arms being turned from bar with spherical knobs turned on in the same way as just described for the banjo connection.

The body should be turned from bar by facing and chamfering one end, drilling and tapping the centre hole and then parting off. A screwed snug or holding piece should then be made in the lathe onto which the body will be screwed and its complete outside form machined to size. If the snug is made from hexagon bar it can then be removed from the lathe and used as a holder for drilling the arm holes. A very light marking out circle can be put on the job while it is still in the lathe. Grip the hexagon of the snug in the drilling vice having first mounted the vice on a taper packing, unless your drilling machine has a tilting table, to give the correct angle of drilling. Use a very small centre drill so that you can accurately pick up your marking line, put in a centre hole and change to a small twist drill with which you can go in the full depth. Finally open out to the correct diameter and then rotate the snug in the vice 180° and repeat the operation.

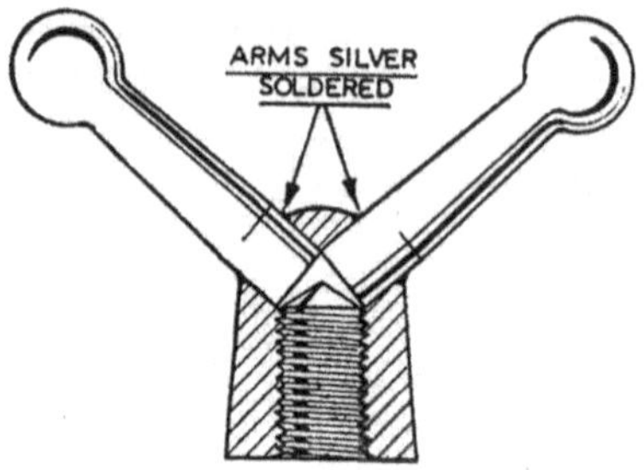

28 *Wing nut for clamping spare wheel*

The wing nut can now be assembled and silver soldered together using "Easy-flo" solder and flux for a really good job. You will now be able to send the nut away to the platers without any need to touch it with hand tools at all.

It would be very easy to fill a complete book with descriptions of parts that can be made in a home workshop but all we can hope to do is perhaps whet your appetite for having a go at making your own parts instead of being dependant on outside sources. The examples we have chosen are all very simple pieces, but many of the principles involved are useful on the more complicated jobs. The great thing to remember is that every job can be broken down into a number of simple operations, most of which can be done on the machines we have described. Providing the operations are performed in the correct sequence and care is taken to see that each step has been properly finished before going on to the next, there is no reason why the amateur cannot make just as good a job as his professional counterpart, even though he will naturally take longer due to lack of practice.

* * *

Here's wishing you many happy hours in your car and in your workshop.

APPENDIX I

Names and Addresses of Recommended Firms

Name	*Address*	*Service or Product*
Abingdon, King Dick, Ltd.	Abingdon Works, Kings Road, Birmingham, 11.	Spanners.
Amal Ltd.	Holford Road, Witton, Birmingham, 6.	Control joints.
George Angus Ltd.	Oil Seals Division, Coast Road, Wallsend-on-Tyne, Northumberland.	Oil seals.
Associated Engineering (Sales) Ltd.	Highgate Road, Birmingham, 12.	Pistons, rings, gudgeon-pins, circlips, liners.
Automotive Products Ltd.	Tachbrook Road, Leamington Spa, Warwickshire.	Hydraulic brakes and clutches.
Bailey and Mackey Ltd.	7 Baltimore Road, Birmingham, 22.	Pressure gauges.
Basset Down Farms Ltd. (Engineering).	Basset Down, Nr. Swindon, Wilts.	Complete restorations.
G. Becktel Ltd.	35 Carver Street, Birmingham, B1 3AT	Screws, nuts, washers, bolts, spring washers, split pins.
A. H. Bedford and Son Ltd.	The Corn Exchange, Team Street, Tenbury Wells, Worcestershire.	Dial painting.
Borg-Warner Ltd.	Letchworth, Herts.	Inverted tooth silent chain and roller chain.
Bosch Ltd.	P.O. Box 166, Rhodes Way, Watford, Herts.	Electrical equipment.
G. F. Bridges Ltd.	Humpage Road, Bordesley Green, Birmingham, 9.	Nuts, screws, washers and bolts, rivets and Helicoil inserts.
Brireten Engineering Ltd.	Brireten Street, Walsall, Staffs.	Machined parts, hardening, grinding, gear cutting.
Britachrome Ltd.	Cope Street, Birmingham, 18.	Hard chrome plating.
B.B.A. Group Ltd.	Cleckheaton, Yorks.	Brake and clutch linings.
British Piston Ring Co. Ltd.	Holbrook Lane, Coventry.	Cast-iron bar.
British Springs Ltd.	Duaflex Works, Oldbury Road, Birmingham, 40.	Road springs.
Brown and Cook Ltd.	37 Ludgate Hill, Birmingham, 3.	Upholstery supplies.
Brylite Batteries Ltd.	Facet Road, Birmingham, 20.	Wood-cased batteries.
W. H. M. Burgess Ltd.	Brunel Road, Old Oak Common Lane, East Acton, London, W.3.	S.U. carburetters, post-1930.
W. Canning and Co. Ltd.	Great Hampton Street, Birmingham, 18.	Skalene descaler.
Chas. Cantrill Ltd.	69 Carver Street, Birmingham, 1.	Cork clutch relining, cork washers.
Central Wheel Co. Ltd.	Lichfield Road, Water Orton, Warwickshire.	Wire wheel rebuilding.
City of Birmingham Workshop for the Blind.	62 Woodville Road, Birmingham, 17.	Coconut mats.

APPENDIX I

Name	*Address*	*Service or Product*
Clayton, Dewandre Co. Ltd.	Titanic Works, Lincoln.	Vacuum servo motors.
Commercial Ignition Co. Ltd.	Longfield Works, Denham, Middlesex.	Bosch magneto and electrical equipment overhauls.
Commercial X-Rays Ltd.	Foundry Lane, Birmingham, 40.	X-ray and crack detecting.
Complete Automobilist Ltd.	39 Main Street, Baston, Nr. Peterborough.	Vintage bodywork and electrical accessories.
Connolly Bros. (Curriers) Ltd.	Chalton Street, London, N.W.1.	Leatherwork renovation.
Cooper & Co. Ltd.	Brynmawr, Breconshire.	Felt washers.
T. D. Cross and Sons Ltd.	Shady Lane, Birmingham, 22b.	Sprockets.
Joseph Dixon Tool Co. Ltd.	Bott Lane, Walsall, Staffs.	Bone folders.
Dunbar and Cook Ltd.	107 New John Street, Birmingham, 6.	Balancing.
Charles Eades Ltd.	New Summer Street, Birmingham, 19.	Engraving.
W. G. Eaton.	18 Freeman Street, Birmingham, 5.	Leather clutch linings, belting and straps.
Electric Service Co. (B'ham) Ltd.	32 Lower Essex Street, Birmingham, 5.	Electrical repairs and supplies.
Enfield Auto Electrical Ltd.	61 Main Avenue, Bush Hill Park, Enfield, Middlesex.	Magneto and electrical equipment overhaul.
Enots Ltd.	Aston Brook Street, Birmingham, 6.	Pipe fittings, filler caps and drain plugs.
Exceloid Ltd.	Greenhoughs Row, Lichfield, Staffs.	Steering-wheel covering.
Fergus Engineering Ltd.	Dorrington, Spalding, Lincs.	Complete restorations.
William Gabb Ltd.	127 Barr Street, Birmingham, 19.	Non-ferrous metals.
Hallam, Sleigh & Cheston Ltd.	Widney Works, Bagot Street, Birmingham, 4.	Coachbuilders' suppliers.
Hardy Spicer Ltd.	Chester Road, Birmingham, 24.	Propeller-shafts.
Heat Treatments Ltd.	Holford Road, Birmingham, 6.	Heat treatment.
Heaven Dowsett and Co. Ltd.	197 Shady Lane, Birmingham, 22a.	Tufnol, ebonite and plastics.
J. A. Hemming Ltd.	Pelsall Road, Brownhills, Staffs.	Shim steel.
H. M. Hobson Ltd.	Fordhouses, Wolverhampton.	Telegauge repairs.
Hofmann and Burton Ltd.	Fairfield Works, Reading Road, Henley-on-Thames, Oxon.	Engine and complete car overhaul, respling of hubs.
Hopton & Sons Ltd.	Union Works, Market Harborough, Leics.	Bent ash hoodsticks.
Hurst Hill Enamel Co. Ltd.	Biddings Lane, Deepfields, Nr. Bilston, Staffs.	Vitreous enamel.
Albert Jagger Ltd.	Green Lane, Walsall, Staffs.	Coachbuilders' supplies.
W. G. James Ltd.	Starts Hill Avenue, Farnborough, Orpington, Kent.	Valves.
Jenolite Ltd.	Boundary House, Boston Road, London, W.7.	Jenolite.
Johnson Matthey and Co. Ltd.	65 Vittoria Street, Birmingham, 1.	Silver solder.
Kayser, Ellison and Co. Ltd.	Carlisle Steel Works, Sheffield, 5.	Alloy steels.
A. J. Lander & Co. Ltd.	55 Stanhope St., Birmingham, 12.	Metal spinnings.

APPENDIX I

Name	*Address*	*Service or Product*
Latex Cushion Co. Ltd.	830 Kingsbury Road, Birmingham, 24.	Latex foam cushions.
Laystall Engineering Co. Ltd.	53 Great Suffolk Street, London, S.E.1.	Brake-drum lining and crank balancing.
W. Lewthwaite and Sons Ltd.	15 Belmont Row, Birmingham, 4.	Inverted tooth silent chains and roller chains.
Lifford Engineering Co. Ltd.	47B Factory Centre, Kings Norton, Birmingham, 30.	Engine and complete car overhaul. Reboring, crank grinding. Polishing, plating, stove enamelling.
Marples and Beasley Ltd.	5 South Road, Birmingham, 19.	Enamelled badge repairs.
Metal Treatments Ltd.	86 Heathmill Lane, Birmingham, 9.	Stove enamelling.
Metallisation Ltd.	Pear Tree Lane, Dudley, Staffs.	Metal spraying.
Metalock (Britain) Ltd.	Grand Buildings, Trafalgar Square, London, W.C.2.	Metalock casting repair.
Joseph Nichols and Sons, Ltd.	Cheapside Works, Birmingham, 12.	Wire stone guards.
Northampton Autorads Ltd.	39 Regent Square, Northampton.	Radiator and petrol tank repairs.
R. H. Nuttall Ltd.	97 St. Clements Road, Birmingham, 7.	Leather and fibre washers.
E. Perkins and Co. Ltd.	19 Selborne Street, Walsall, Staffs.	Plastic knobs.
Arthur Price Ltd.	Vevo Works, Park Lane, Birmingham, 6.	Windscreens.
Quality Springs and Productions Ltd.	St. Georges Road, Redditch.	Springs other than road springs.
Ram Research Ltd.	Susan Wood, Chislehurst, Kent, BR7 5RD.	Hot paint.
Renold Ltd.	Renold Works, Didsbury, Manchester.	Roller chains.
Thomas Richfield and Son Ltd.	Broadstone Place, Blandford Street, London, W.1.	Bowden cables.
Ripaults Ltd.	Southbury Road, Enfield, Middx.	Armoured electrical cable.
Rocol Ltd.	Rocol House, Swillington, Nr. Leeds.	Heavy gear oil, anti-scuffing paste.
Rubery Owen and Co. Ltd.	Chassis Repair Section, Meeting Street, Wednesbury, Staffs.	Chassis frame repairs.
Rudders & Paynes Ltd.	Hollies Avenue, Cannock, Staffs.	Timber supplies and bent ash hoodsticks.
Llewellyn Ryland Ltd.	Balsall Heath, Birmingham, 12.	Paint and varnish.
George Salter and Co. Ltd.	High Street, West Bromwich, Staffs.	Flexible roller bearings.
Schofield and Samson Ltd.	Spencer Works, Roger Street, London, W.C.1.	Gear wheels.
Silentbloc Ltd.	Manor Royal, Crawley, Sussex.	Silentbloc flexible bearings.
C. E. Smith Ltd.	82 Franchise Street, Birmingham, 22b.	Reboring, crank grinding, balancing.
J. E. Smith.	24 Lyndon Croft, Marston Green, Birmingham.	Magneto repairs.
Sorber Accessories Ltd.	16a Osten Mews, South Kensington, London, S.W.7.	Reconditioning of Hartford shock absorbers.
Speedometer Supply Co. Ltd.	34 Shelton Street, London, W.C.2.	Speedometer and tachometer repairs.

APPENDIX I

Name	*Address*	*Service or Product*
Springfield Wheel Co. Ltd.	155 Springfield Road, Birmingham, 8.	Wire wheel rebuilding.
S.U. Carburetter Co. Ltd.	Wood Lane, Birmingham, 24.	Pre-1930 S.U. carburetter repairs.
Herbert Terry and Sons Ltd.	Redditch, Worcester.	Valve springs.
Tool Treatments (Chemical) Ltd.	Colliery Road, Birmingham Road, West Bromwich, Staffordshire.	Chemical black.
G. H. Turner & Co. Ltd.	Pountney Street, Wolverhampton.	Gear cutting.
Venesta (Veneers) Ltd.	Hayseech Road, Halesowen, Staffs.	Hardwood veneers.
Vintage Racing Cars Ltd.	Derby Road Garage, Northampton.	Autovac repairs and spares.
Vintage Tyre Supplies Ltd.	Jackman Mews, Neasden, London, N.W.10.	Beaded edge and Vintage sizes of tire.
James Walker and Co. Ltd.	Depots throughout the world.	Copper and asbestos gaskets, Gaskoid and Nebar jointing materials.
Walker Spencer Components Ltd.	5 High Street, Birmingham, 14.	Nuts, screws, washers and bolts.
Walsall Locks and Cart Gear Ltd.	Neale Street, Walsall, Staffs.	Door locks.
A. P. Warren Ltd.	37 Sheen Road, Richmond, Surrey.	Stud extractor.
West London Repair Co. Ltd.	5 Lancaster Road, Wimbledon, London, S.W.19.	Wheel rebuilding and road spring reconditioning.
T. Whittle and Sons Ltd.	Rose and Crown Street, Warrington, Lancashire.	Whittle belts.
Wilcot (Parent) Co. Ltd.	Fishponds, Bristol.	Leather gaiters.
I. Wilkinson and Son Ltd.	Stafford Street, Derby.	Coachwork restoration.
F. B. Willmott Ltd.	36 River Street, Birmingham, 5.	Starter rings.
Jonas Woodhead Ltd.	Kirkstall Road, Leeds.	Road springs.
Jonas Woodhead and Son (Scotland) Ltd.	Chapelhall, Lanarkshire.	Hartford shock-absorber repairs.
Woodstock Weaving Co. Ltd.	Seale Street, Mansfield Road, Derby.	Bonnet tape.
Zenith Carburetter Co. Ltd.	Honeypot Lane, Stanmore, Middx.	Zenith and Solex carburetters.

APPENDIX II

Clubs and Registers Specialising in Vintage and Thoroughbred Motor-Cars

Club or Register	*Address of Secretary*
A.C. Owners Club	28 Downsview Road, Upper Norwood, London, S.E.19.
Aston Martin Owners Club Ltd.	22 The Mall, East Sheen, London, S.W.14.
Alvis Owners Club	31 Pennington Drive, Oatlands Chase, Weybridge, Surrey.
The Alvis Register	'Lawnview', Towpath, Shepperton, Middlesex.
Auburn Cord Duesenberg Club	830 Miranda Green, Palo Alto, Ca. 94306. Maple Rise, Oakhanger-Bordon, Hants, England.
Bentley Drivers Club Ltd.	76a High St., Long Crendon, Aylesbury, Bucks.
B.M.W. Car Club	3 The Avenue, Chinnor, Oxford OX9 4PA.
Bugatti Owners Club	40 Bartholomew St., Newbury, Berks.
Bullnose Morris Club	3 Glebe Lane, Great Shelford, Cambridge.
Citroen Car Club	32 Lower Road, Fetcham, Leatherhead, Surrey.
Delage Owners Club and Register	6 Hillbrow Road, Withdean, Brighton, Sussex.
Fiat Car Club of Great Britain	The Mount, Willingham Road, Lea, Gainsborough, Lincs.
Fiat Motor Club (G.B.)	3 Woodfield Road, Ashtead, Surrey.
Fiat Register	Dickenson and Norris Ltd., Melton Mowbray, Leicestershire.
Frazer-Nash Car Club	Shellingford House, Nr. Faringdon, Berks.
20 Ghost Club	Aldwick Hundred, Aldwick, Sussex.
Les Hommes a L'Hispano	37 St. James Place, London. S.W.1.
Humber Register (1900–1930)	108 Barnett Wood Lane, Ashtead, Surrey.
Lagonda Club	35 Cobbold Ave., Eastbourne, Sussex.
Lancia Motor Club	10 Arthur Road, Motspur Road, New Malden, Surrey.
Lea-Francis Owners Club	105 Boxley Drive, West Bridgford, Nottingham, NG2 7GN
Mercedes-Benz Club	Hollyhurst House, Barton-under-Needwood, Staffs.
M.G. Car Club	c/o The M.G. Car Co. Ltd., Abingdon-on-Thames, Berks.
Rapier Register	7 Gray's Walk, Druids Green, Cowbridge, Glam.
Renault Owners Club	15 Lowshoe Lane, Romford, Essex.
Riley Motor Club	Riley Motors Ltd., Abingdon-on-Thames, Oxon.
Riley Register	162 Leicester Road, Glenhills, Leicester.
Rover Sports Register	11 Woodhall Drive, Pinner, Middlesex.
British Salmson Owners Club	14 Rowhill Crescent, Aldershot, Hants.
French Salmson Register	Apple Tree Cottage, Rectory Close, Ashtead, Surrey.
Singer Owners Club	31 Rivershill, Watton-at-Stone, Hertford.
Sunbeam S.T.D. Register	5 Wood Lodge, Wimbledon, London, S.W.19.
Sunbeam-Talbot Owners Club	Ladbroke Hall, Barlby Road, London, W.10.
Vintage Sports Car Club Ltd.	Bone Lane, Newbury, Berks.

INDEX

The numerals in **heavy type** refer to the *figure numbers* of drawings in the text